THE BAREFOOT
CUE BALL

If you want to learn the intricacies of pool, from beginning to end, read this book. "Doc" Rutter is a Master of explanation.
        Conrad Burkman, Retired publisher of, "The National Billiard News"

Billiard knowledge obtained from Doc, thirty years ago has stood the test of time. The information in this book is explained clearly and is easily understood. The idiosyncrasies of the game became compelling to me. I will be eternally grateful to him for this revelation.
  "**Ty**" **Wilson**, multiple State Masters team Champion, 7 time **National** VNEA & BCA Team Champion,

I will keep on reading this book as it makes me play better than ever and it makes things simple to me. Doc knows and is able to explain pool better than anyone I know. If it wasn't for him, I would probably not be playing now!
  Wayne "The Rosedale Flash", (Who plays for Cash $), Miller, Multiple State Team Champion in both Minnesota and Wisconsin, Master league MVP 2011, 6th in BCA Senior Division Nationals at The Riviera in 2011

Finally, an enjoyable book that tells you WHY the balls do what they do. It leaves you with a smirk of understanding, on your face rather than scratching your head in ignorance. Doc makes the complex fun and easy to grasp and gives you a better understanding of some things you thought you already knew.
  "**Fast Freddy**" **Lamers**, Minnesota Billiard Club, Regional 3 cushion Champion, & Minnesota State Team Champion

Doc Rutter is one of the best-known, best liked, and best informed teachers of the game. Read this book and you'll see why—Here are the lessons of a lifetime presented in a readable style.
  Robert Byrne, Author of seven internationally distributed Billiard books, and member of the Billiard Congress of America Hall-Of-Fame

In the mid-eighties I took Doc's private instruction and went from a recreational player to a State Team Championship in 1990. Doc teaches the cue ball physics in simple terms and makes it look easy.
  Denny "The Dawg" Amundson, Minnesota State Team Champion, 1990

I like this book!! Doc taught me to develop a game plan, starting with the eight ball and working backwards. I remember thinking, "Is he nuts"?? Well it worked, and all the other tips & strategies he covered with me, also worked.
  Shawn "Double Jump" Oglesbee, Minnesota State Team Champion

THE BAREFOOT CUE BALL

An easy entry into the magic world of cue ball manipulation and some entertaining pool stories.

Paul A. "Doc" Rutter

authorHOUSE®

AuthorHouse™
1663 Liberty Drive
Bloomington, IN 47403
www.authorhouse.com
Phone: 1-800-839-8640

© 2011 by Paul A. "Doc" Rutter. All rights reserved.

No part of this book may be reproduced, stored in a retrieval system, or transmitted by any means without the written permission of the author.

First published by AuthorHouse   10/28/2011

ISBN: 978-1-4670-3901-7 (sc)
ISBN: 978-1-4670-3899-7 (ebk)

Library of Congress Control Number: 2011916947

Printed in the United States of America

Any people depicted in stock imagery provided by Thinkstock are models, and such images are being used for illustrative purposes only.
Certain stock imagery © Thinkstock.

This book is printed on acid-free paper.

Because of the dynamic nature of the Internet, any web addresses or links contained in this book may have changed since publication and may no longer be valid. The views expressed in this work are solely those of the author and do not necessarily reflect the views of the publisher, and the publisher hereby disclaims any responsibility for them.

Contents

Two Disclaimers 2
Style 3
The "Bare-Foot" Cue Ball 3
Ahem, Does This Microphone Work 3
Pocketing Balls 4
Physics 4
Energy Management 5

Stopping The Cue Ball 7

Side Spin, On The Cue Ball 11
Observing Some More Physics 13
Drawing The Cue Ball 14
Short Power Draws 16

More Cloth Tricks 19
Relaxed Draw 19
Ninety-Miles Per Hour 20
Fun With Relaxed Draw And Some Other Stuff 22
More Dead Ball Stuff 23
Adding Spin 25
Learn By Watching, Now 26

Some Cue Ball Magic 28
Body Lock Stance 29
Natural Slip Stroke 30
Jacked UP Cue Stick 31
Masse 32
More Balls And Cloth Info 33
Squirt 35
Bohemian-Gypsy Curse Of Knowledge 37
Practice 38

Practice Drills 41
Around The English Clock 42
Jumping The Cue Ball 42
Spins And Throws 43
Push Throw 45
Dead Combinations 46
Multiple Ball Throws 46
Frozen Kiss Shots 47
Unfrozen Kiss Shots 49
My Nemesis Kiss Shot 50
Inertia 50
More Energy Management Stuff 51
Eight Ball Pattern Shooting 53
Back To The Pattern Test 56
Practice Pattern Drill 58
Banking 59
Pinch Bank 62
A Simple Three-Rail Education 63
Small Table Eight Ball America's Game 65

Minor Strategies And Spurious Info 68
Jedi Mind Trick 71
Focus 72
Pause Stroke 73
The Zone 74

Incentive 76

Break Shots 78
Rack Your Own 81

Straight Pool 83
The Quadrant Theory 84

Safety Play 88

Personal Instruction 91
Three Cushion 92

Strategies 93

Social Order, Girls And Leagues 95

Dress Codes 97

Poolroom Etiquette 99
Zanesville, Ohio, The Arcade Poolroom 99

Billiard Life Influences 100
Martha M. Rutter, My Martie 100
Duard Schmelke... 100
Arved "Red" Jones.. 101
The Rutters 101
Bill "Weenie Beanie" Staton 102
Luther "Wimpy" Lassiter 103
Conrad Burkman 104
George Fels 104
Robert Byrne.. 105
Nick Varner.. 105
Cecil "Buddy" Hall 105
Robert Runde... 106
Jimmy 'The Kid' Wetch 106
Jackie Gleason & Paul Newman 107
Jesse Engel.. 107
Phil Capelle.. 107
Things I Learned, Just Watching 108

Pool Stories I Must Share... 111
Spring Lake Park, Minnesota.. 111
Las Vegas, Nevada, The Riviera Casino 111
Somerset, Wisconsin, Rendezvous Bar................................ 112
Somewhere In The Usa 112
Louisville, Kentucky, The Executive West Hotel................. 112
The Poolroom Philosophy, Adapted By "Doc" Rutter 113

This is not a book for beginners. It is written primarily for those players who think they already know how to play. However it is easy to read, so be brave, and have at it.

Some of those players may be looking for that little something extra. There are things going on right under a player's nose that they may only be vaguely aware of. I am covering those "Secrets" that you need to know in today's competitive world.

There are many good, even great "How To" Billiard instruction books available for today's players that contain the nitty-gritty details that pool players thrive on.

Robert Byrne wrote seven Billiard books, and the first one, is titled the "Standard Book of Pool And Billiards". The illustrations and explanations are excellent. I recommend it as a, must have, very good reference.

My approach is a little more offbeat. Some parts are technical; some parts mystical, and narrative, with both a serious aim, and a lighter, good-old-boy, flavor.

Some small, real life, or billiard experience stories are included, to help make a point or just to amuse you.

Some of my psychobabble with Jedi Knight, semi-amusing, references will appeal to the spiritual, sub-conscious parts of your mind. At the same time there is technical information that will appeal to your mechanical skills thought process.

I suggest you keep a copy of Bob's book beside your practice table for quick technical and/or illustrated reference. His illustrations are very good.

If you stay with me to the end of this, you will realize, that you have become, somewhat like Yoda. You will be **your own teacher**, and will probably not have to ask questions again as you can now figure out situations for yourself. These writings will teach you how to **think** about your pool game as much as how to play. If nothing else, you can retell some of the stories to your poolroom friends.

We have passed through one of the greatest billiard, High Interest, time periods of the recent era. This period was inspired by the 1987 movie, "The Color Of Money".

This period started in the fall of 1987, burst through the 1990's and then trickled into the early 2000's.

Yes the interest has waned. The younger crowd today couldn't care less about playing pool. It is much too hard to learn and their interest is taken by the, cell phone, text-messaging fad. Pool just doesn't have the "I must do it as everyone else is" social impact, that "Color of Money" created.

The kids are fine. They are smart and easy to converse with; they just are not inspired to play pool.

The billiard world today survives on the hardcore League and Local Tournament players that are left over from the movie inspired pool boom. These players still have to have their weekly fix of pool playing activity. This group is slowly aging, but as they get older, their experience has made them better players. The camaraderie and respect that permeates the billiard activity in this group is enjoyable to experience.

I have enjoyed discussing (debating), billiard strategy and mind set with some of our great and varied aficionados, even if we just end up telling wonderful ageless pool stories.

If you must share a pool story, I am the old curmudgeon, up there in the "Cheap Seats". Come on up, sit down, and tell me your tale, but please don't tell me about your uncle, cousin, or grandpa that beat Mosconi years ago. I have heard that lie so many times that I wonder if poor Willie ever beat anybody, ha.

Another often repeated gem is how dozens of my casual pool playing acquaintances, or customers, "Hustled" their way through college.

Alas, the first liar doesn't have a chance, and atmosphere comes in many scents, and colors.

TWO DISCLAIMERS

I respect the women in our Game/Sport, but I am not going through the tiresome, politically correct, he/she gender reference every time it comes up. I will use He, Him, or Player. If you are female, please mentally insert your own gender in the proper place. I have a great respect for Allison Fisher, and I don't want her admonishing me.

STYLE

You will observe that I write with "Style and Grace". The Style is pure "Ohio River Valley Redneck". The Grace comes from my Bohemian, and Scotch-Irish ancestry.

For your edification, a Bohemian is a Gypsy, with a job, and puzzled about it.

I will use Quote marks excessively and some Redneck country boy slang on occasion, and Capitals where ever I choose to put them, for some slight emphasis.

THE "BARE-FOOT" CUE BALL

When you get down to the nitty-gritty, and take the Shoes and Socks off the cue ball, we find that, **" The Bare-Foot Cue Ball, Is The Game"**.

Players are lead astray by the relatively easy job of shooting the object ball into a pocket. Then they think, I am playing now, "How much more would I have to know", to be a great player? It is impossible to imagine something that you don't know!

In the Twin City area of Minnesota, some local players know the cue ball as "Mel", short for Melbert. This info is good for Friday night Bar-Bets and general, half inebriated arguments. The real secret to pocket billiard success is to Control "Mel". We all know **easy shots are easy shots.** If a player can learn how to play **superior position**, then the object ball shots are easier; hence we now start to look like a really good player.

Gee, and you thought this would be difficult. Well, there is a lot of info that you are going to have to absorb and methods to practice. Let's get started.

As a player of experience, by now you have read a few books on the subject and have viewed some instructional videos. You may have learned a great deal that, just maybe, you don't completely understand. With the shoes & socks out of the way, just how, exactly, does the Cue Ball work? I'm going to tell yah!! Read on Cashmere.

AHEM, DOES THIS MICROPHONE WORK

The game of Pocket Billiards is a combination of complications. It is a direct application of Physics and Artistry, tied together with your logical and emotional, "Jedi Knight" mysticism. *All great players Slide the cue ball, in some fashion. The cue ball only rolls after the kinetic energy wears off. That concept will be elaborated on, in various forms throughout this book*

The mystery & magic of the cue ball is what keeps the players intrigued by the billiard games throughout their lifetime. Never bored, nevermore.

The speeds and spins that can be applied to the cue ball, are infinitely variable, within the friction range of the cue balls spherical surface.

The game is not constructed of big **cement blocks** of knowledge, but is more like a pile of sand. Many, many little pieces of knowledge that have to be each assembled in different, variable sized groups, for each separate task that is to be accomplished at each separate time. I wish that I could make it easier.

POCKETING BALLS

First major item is pocketing balls. If you are having trouble pocketing balls, take up tennis, checkers or that cash absorbing, "Black Hole", Texas Hold-um poker.

After the ghost cue ball method of pocketing balls is shown to you and you are in the ballpark, it is trial and error. Start with short shots and as you get better, work up to harder ones. Most players show a natural, ball pocketing talent. You most likely have been there and are past that by now.

PHYSICS

Don't panic, this is the most sophisticated word I will use in this friendly diatribe. I promise to avoid "Tangent Lines, Fortuitous, Disingenuous and Fruition", and other such Media Speak.

Normal Cast Phenolic balls are two and one quarter inches in diameter and weigh six ounces. There are no significant differences, other than color and the regulation cue balls are the same. These balls are tough and you can bounce them off of a smooth concrete floor.

This sameness relationship between the cue ball, and the object balls is what allows you, by the use of the basic Physics Phenomenon, inherent in these round objects, to have much more control of your position play, than you, at first, realize.

Note. Nonstandard balls of other sizes, weights or materials will require some common sense modifications to your playing application. Ivory, metal—flake, or oversize balls will give different results but may be workable with enough practice.

Different materials will provide different physics characteristics. Various cue balls have decidedly different resilience and as a results play much differently while appearing to look similar.

ENERGY MANAGEMENT

Two sources of energy are applied directly to the cue ball by hitting it with a cue stick. They are, (1) the driven "Kinetic" energy, and (2) the spin energy. High or low spin only.

Right or left spin on the cue ball doesn't add or take away energy, **(it just confuses the object ball).**

High or low spin applied to the cue ball, will alter the exit path of the cue ball after contact with the object ball.

Line up five object balls and freeze them to the foot rail, then with one hand slam the cue ball into the end of this line of balls. You will observe that only one ball goes flying into the corner pocket, and it travels at about the same speed that the cue ball was traveling when it arrived. This is a basic physics phenomenon. The mass out of the impact zone equals the mass in.

You may notice some slight movement of the next to last ball in this line. This is due to the resilience of the cue ball. The phenolic plastic used to make the balls, gets very slightly compressed by the impact with the object balls. That slight compression, then releases immediately after impact, and causes the other balls slight movement. Clay balls don't do this.

It is an action that has almost no bearing on the big picture, and is considered insignificant. Since it occurs, I have taken the time to explain it. It does have a direct bearing on jumping the Cue Ball.

A mass driven into the pile of balls, by your hand power, will cause a mass of an equal amount to pass, through and out of the pile of balls, no more, no less.

The cue balls energy is transferred, for our purpose of explanation, 100% through the pack of balls. The speed, in this short distance, is also consistent.

Other than some microscopic drag from the cloth, our incoming cue ball's speed is also transferred; let's say 99.5% through the pack of balls.

This information will probably make you wonder about breaking a rack of balls.

When you hit a break shot, all you have to work with is the mass and weight of that one ball. The only variable that you can influence is the speed. That one ball's mass and weight is scattered throughout the pack. This is why a tight rack is desired, so the energy flow is uniform. I don't know who is in charge of the actual energy sharing, as it happens too fast to see, ha.

If you continue this basic experiment by hitting with two balls in, you will observe, two balls fly out. Three balls in gets you three balls out. It is important to do this so your subconscious mind forms a picture and the relative power transfer of this, mass in, same mass out, action.

By now a glimmering of the cue ball's power and your job of expending and controlling that power during a normal shot is starting to form. During any shot, you will expend some, or most all, of the cue ball's energy into an object ball. The rest of that cue ball's energy is absorbed by, the other balls, the rails, and/or just runs out of gas, on the cloth's path to infinity.

This also helps explain why some of your cluster or break shots are not always as effective as you had anticipated.

STOPPING THE CUE BALL

You must learn to stop the cue ball. If you can't, stop reading now and give up the game. This is the ground floor of cue ball control and all else is based on this one simple act. Physics dictates that only one way works consistently.

You must, with your dead level, consistent stroke, (which you have been working on); slide the cue ball straight into an object ball. You do this by striking the cue ball 100% in the middle, (up & down, at the equator) and then hit your object ball 100% in the middle (side to side).

If you do that correctly, the cue ball has to stop dead, every time. All of the cue ball's kinetic energy has just been absorbed by the object ball, which you just shot in, hence no energy left, in the cue ball, no more movement is possible.

Any deviation, up, or down, on the cue ball, or sideways, on the object ball, will cause the cue ball to roll, back up or go sideways, which are unsatisfactory results.

The physics phenomenon transfers the energy 100% from the cue ball to the object ball. We have established that the balls are equal in size and weight. Since all the energy is transfer 100% and there is no spin energy applied the cue ball must, and will stop dead, just like it died!!!

Many players during their uneducated previous play have learned to hit the ball below center (somewhere) and then try to estimate how hard or soft to stroke it to try to make the cue ball stop. This method will only be about 80% effective.

By using the correct way, you become about 99.5% effective. Okay, I am allowing for an occasional 0.5% mistake on your part.

At one of the "Bank & One Pocket" Hall-Of-Fame dinners, during the Derby City Classic, several players were telling stories about a great young player from around San Francisco. This player had died young. One of his great strengths that the players were expounding on was his ability to "kill" his cue ball in all different type of shots.

He obviously understood the physics of what I am explaining to you here. Absorb the cue ball's energy and it doesn't get away from you.

Back up a second or two. Think about the relative Honesty of the cue ball. It is not like your high school girl friend. The cue ball cannot and will not lie to you, Huzzah.

After shooting a few of these, if you notice that your cue ball drifts slightly to the right on most of them? Then trust your cue ball. You must be hitting the object ball slightly on the right.

Did you notice it rolling slightly forward on some of them? Trust your cue ball. You are either putting just a little bit of high English on the stroke or you are hitting it too soft and the cloth is giving you just a bit of forward roll, which is a form of high English.

To make the cue ball stop, you must develop the discipline to always hit the cue ball hard enough to *slide* it to the object ball with no spin.

The cloth rubbing on the bottom of the ball is always there, working against you, unless you get smart enough to make it work for you.

Learn to control the physics of this ball & cloth friction action.

Start with short shots. Don't hit three, to, five shots and think you have got it mastered. No, no, Cashmere, this is where the artistry and the sub-conscious mind training comes into play. You have to shoot dozens and eventually hundreds of these at various distances to teach yourself the **"Feel"** of this stroke. Sliding the cue ball, under your control to make it do what you want off the face of the object ball. Check out the illustration below.

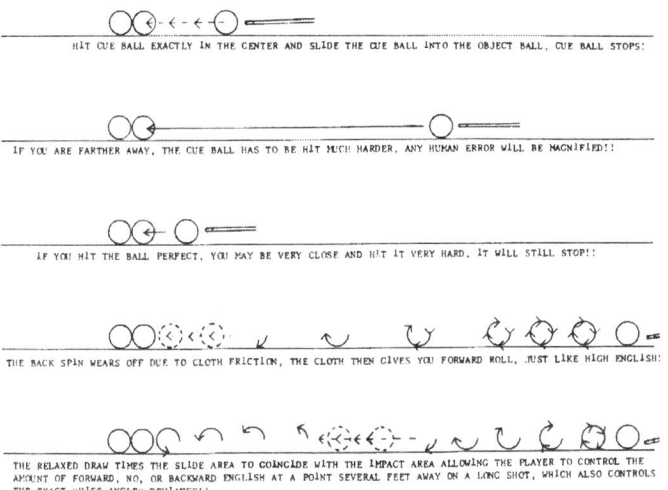

5 lines of sliding cue balls

NOTE. Every section of this document can be elaborated on with fine-tuning and further explanation. I have tried to explain each section to the point that you have enough information to understand what I am trying to teach with out speechifying and boring you to tears. If you need further info on any part, E-Mail your question to (docshot08@msn.com)

When you are in your local poolroom, game room or bowling alley, and you and your friend/opponent are playing for the imaginary Tuesday afternoon 8-ball championship of the World, you must know how the required stroke "FEELS". Shot by shot, there is no "Mulligan", (a free replacement shot) given. You get one chance, each time, to get it right.

After you screw it up, all the long-winded explanations in the world, of what you know and what you intended to do is just so much, "Who Shot John". You and your opponent and the Tuesday afternoon sideline game Sweaters all know it.

Paul A. "Doc" Rutter

However the well practiced, and well-executed, proper shot/stroke speaks silent volumes about you're abilities to all the "Cheap Seat Critics" watching. Now think about the pros and cons of that, Herschel.

SIDE SPIN, ON THE CUE BALL

If your target ball is close to a pocket, you can probably use a lot of sidespin, and since you are close to a rail, the sidespin will be visually dramatic, and effective, and you will get away with it.

As your target ball gets farther and farther away from the pocket, your shot pocketing error angle diminishes.

You must be more accurate just to pocket the ball. The amount of throw transferred to the target ball, by the sidespin, on the cue ball, is inconsistent, and may be difficult, or impossible to estimate. (See spin throws later)

A rule of thumb is, if an object ball is close to a pocket, gamble, go for it, but as your target ball gets farther away from the pocket, tone down your risks, with very little or no side spin.

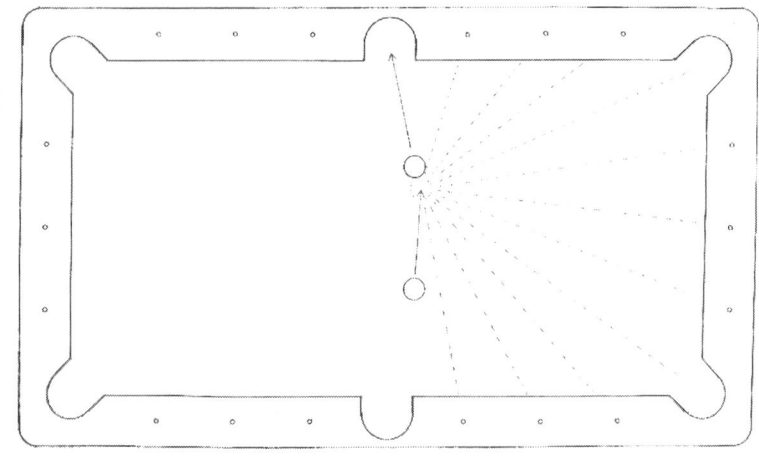

Spray shot

This exercise will prove the power of high and low English on the cue ball. Lay your cue stick across the side pockets just over the right side corners at the edge of the side pockets. Place two pieces of chalk under the cue stick, about a third of the way across the table. Remove the cue stick. Push down on the chalks and spin a mark down into the cloth, leaving a blue swirl mark under each chalk. These marks easily brush away. Remove the chalks. Put your cue ball on the mark closest to you and an object ball on the mark the farthest away. Now wouldn't it be a miracle if you could shoot that ball into the side pocket across from you and make the cue ball go to all of the designated paths, shown by the dotted lines in the illustration.

Not only can I do it, but also I will explain it so you can learn how to do it. Start at the top of the cue ball with as much topspin as your imagination will allow.

Shoot three or four shots, and observe the cue ball's exit path. Now with everything the same, lower your cue tip slightly. Hit three or four more shots at this new lower cue tip position.

Do you see any difference in the cue ball's exit path? Go back to the same shot, lower the cue tip a little bit more and shoot three or four shots at this new height. See another difference in the cue ball's exit path?

Each different cue tip position applies a different rate of spin to the cue ball. That rate of spin determines the cue ball's exit path from the object ball.

Continue to lower the cue tip and monitor the resultant changes in the cue ball's exit paths for each different English height. Try to maintain the approximate same speed.

Since you are shooting a ball that is almost straight in, your kinetic energy is mostly being absorbed into the object ball, and your spin is affecting the cue ball's exit path by a large amount.

Hi, Teach, learning anything? This effect is there for every cut shot you shoot, but as the cut gets thinner, the spin control lessens, due to less kinetic energy being absorbed into the object ball. DO NOT use any sidespin. Inadvertently you may not shoot the object ball to the same part of the pocket each time. This will add an additional, small variation to the cue ball's exit angle. This variation is another tool for you to use

OBSERVING SOME MORE PHYSICS

When you hit the cue ball it doesn't roll. What? That's right. The cue ball usually slides for the first part, of its journey. Sooner or later the cloth drag causes it to pick up a forward roll and it will roll the rest of the way until it stops.

If the ball hits a rail, in it's travels, it may also pick up some sidespin. While the cue ball is sliding, it may be also be spinning in some direction as the player had applied that spin with the cue stick.

Control of this sliding feature is the phenomenal artistic power that separates the "PLAYERS" from the "players".

It may sound like I am avoiding a rolling ball, not so. A rolling cue ball has value and may be an asset, but only when it suits the criteria of your shot plan.

Respected billiard author, Mister Robert Byrne advised me that if you hit the cue ball seven tenths up from the exact bottom, it would start out with a normal roll. Thanks Bob.

Load up a side pocket with balls. Practice straight in stop shots by shooting the balls across the table into the other side pocket. When it is full, go over there and shoot them back.

Don't even bother with the cue ball. You may use any of the balls as a cue ball while you are practicing, they are made of the same material and it will not hurt them.

Shoot an object ball and then use the next object ball to shoot the one you just used as a practice cue ball. Remember they are all the same size and weight. By using object balls as a cue ball, you don't have to reset a new object ball, for each shot. You will also get some visual info due to the object balls design.

Continue to shoot the stop shots at various distances, while training your sub-conscious mind what is the feel of this stroke. You are not trying to hit the ball hard or soft as much as you are trying to learn to hit it "Nice".

Your stroke should be such that the cue ball will be half way to the object ball before it realizes that it has been hit!!

A good follow through stroke feels, Nice The more follow through, the "Nicer" it feels. When you start to see the results, it really feels Nice all over better than anywhere else. You have arrived, ha.

Feel your cue stick **PUSH** the cue ball, not hit it or poke it. Hit through the cue ball like you are trying to hit it twice, don't worry, you won't. That is one of the reasons we practice, to try new things, to see how they work and do we want to use them, in our real games.

During your stop shot practices, as your cue ball and object balls get farther apart, you will have to keep adding power or follow through to keep the cue ball from picking up forward roll from the cloth drag. With that big picture in mind keep working on your speed and follow through of stroke.

DRAWING THE CUE BALL

Nothing is more artistically satisfying than a nice draw stroke. Properly executed it gives a player a warm feeling and a sense of satisfaction.

I will just bet that you are not happy with your draw stroke. Famous billiard author, George Fels, started one of his books with sentence, (I paraphrase here), "I'm sorry to tell you that you are probably hitting the balls too hard".

Hit it firm, hit it soft, hit it medium, but hit it Nice. Stroke it with an artistic push. Follow through that cue ball like you are playing a cello, not trying to kill a copperhead snake. Form the mental picture that you are sliding or spinning the cue ball, not rolling it.

I have taught hundreds of fellow pool players, in the Twin-Cities area. I always casually observed their attempts to draw the cue ball.

Most players are scared to hit the cue ball close to the bottom. They may have miscued once or twice and now won't go anywhere near that bottom area of the cue ball again. Other players may have made fun of them, when they miscued or scooped under the ball causing an inadvertent jumped cue ball.

I then proceed to demonstrate, (with my maniacal ego approach) by hitting the cue ball all the way on the bottom, I will deliberately jump the cue ball off of the pool table. I then calmly stand back and point out how, the roof didn't cave in, God didn't strike me dead and that no other damage occurred. I have seen Mike Massey shoot draw shots and leave a chalk trail on the cloth. That is how low he hits the cue ball.

Now is the time to do it wrong so you will know how to do it right. How will you know how low to hit the cue ball until you have tried every position, clear down to the bottom? If you hit the ball S-m-o-o-t-h, you may hit it real low without any trauma, to you or the cue ball. You will only learn by doing.

When you are finished with your stop ball practice, use the same method to practice draws. Fill up the side pocket with balls. Then calmly stroke them into the other side, and back and forth. Make a chalk spin mark and shoot from your marks.

Chalk is important. It is the fine grit, made from sand that makes the friction connection between your smooth leather tip and the smooth plastic ball. Our Bohemian friend in Chicago, Illinois, "Skip" Nemecek, one of the owners of "Tweeten Fibre Co." makes all the "Master and Triangle" chalk you can use and he will sell it to you, "For Cheap" ha. Use it now. Skip is my "Go To Guy" when chalk or cue tip questions come up. He has been supporting the pool players for his whole life.

During play chalk every shot without fail. When I am practicing, I cheat the Chalk Company. When practicing continuous draw shots, I rotate my cue stick slightly, and can get about five or six shots between chalking, don't tell, "Skip". Look at the money I just saved you on chalk, and you thought I was just a pretty face.

When you are practicing, that is the time to hit that cue ball lower, then lower and then lower than that. Using a serious smooth follow through. If you start miscuing consistently, raise up, just a wee bit. The smoother you stroke, the better this works. You can hit the cue ball lower than you have been, if you sneak up on it with a "very smooth stroke". You may hear the words "follow through", but you actually have to do it. When shooting, physically extend your cue stick stroke through the cue ball contact area farther than you normally do. It makes a difference!!!! Then you practice, to learn to control that difference.

You may have found your bottom. Aren't you surprised by now how your draw shots have improved?

It doesn't matter what some local poolroom pseudo-hero can do. What can you do? Your consistency and control in future games and tournaments depend on this.

As you continue to shoot practice draw shots, improve your game power. Start using the diamonds and half diamonds, on the rail, on your side of the table, as targets for the cue ball you are drawing.

First hit the object ball as straight as possible and draw the cue back into the side pocket. Next hit the object ball just a very small amount, (one or two degrees), on the side and observe the cue ball coming back, a small amount, on that side. Now try the other side. You quickly see that any variation of your input makes a definite difference in your cue ball's exit path. Think how great your position power just improved.

SHORT POWER DRAWS

A draw variation that is very valuable goes like this. Line up a shot with a short distance between the balls, about six to eight inches. Line up your cue stick, in the center of the cue ball, as if you are going to hit a stop shot. Now lower your cue stick a fraction, maybe a sixteenth of an inch. Now punch it with some power. You should observe the cue ball comes back to you, not very far but with a certain feel of control. Obviously this is also going to need some practice.

This short "power draw" will allow you to hit some of those position windows that are not very far away, but you don't want to overshoot them.

This same concept works on a short follow shot. Line up your cue tip in the center of the cue ball, up & down, and then raise the tip up a sixteenth or an eighth of an inch. Now punch it. Observe the action and make the appropriate adjustments in cue tip height and shot force, until you get the desired results.

Most players addressing the cue ball are in the middle, or all the way down at the bottom, or all the way up to the top of the cue ball. Hardly ever do they hit the cue ball slightly lower or higher. There is a lot of cue ball power and control waiting for you there. You have to practice these variations before you will understand them.

Look at the illustration below. If you hit the cue ball at an **arbitrary** twenty miles per hour, at each of the different shown cue stick spots, that will give the cue ball a different rate of spin, for each different spot. The different rate of spin will cause the cue ball's exit path, from contact with the target ball, to change direction, on a cut shot.

This is a phenomenon that requires extensive work to build it into your mental position game. The rate of spin, high or low will control the variation of the cue ball, from it's normal exit angle, on every cut shot. Thinner cuts will have very little control; fatter cuts will allow much more control of the cue balls exit angle.

Reference the Spray Shot Illustration.

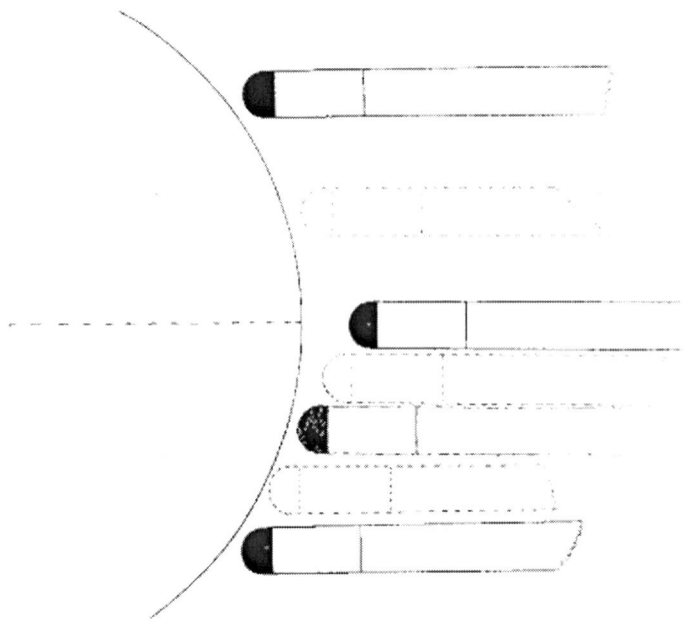

Large cue ball showing 7 different hit spots

MORE CLOTH TRICKS

Clear your table and use about two or three striped balls. Line up the balls about twelve inches from the foot rail and with the stripes facing you horizontally, shoot them down the table, one at a time, several times, using various draw strokes. You should observe that the balls spin backwards for several inches. The cloth wears off the backspin. Then the ball slides for several inches, (3 to 8) depending on the force of stroke. Then the ball starts, and continues to roll until it hits the far rail and comes back

Go back and check the bottom example in the first illustration about stopping the cue ball. (Page 9)

Think about these shots, throughout your billiard career, you have seen this very same action by casually rolling striped balls and you had very little idea that it would or could affect your play. Since the cue ball is white, this effect is usually hidden from you.

RELAXED DRAW

Now place an object ball close to a corner pocket and in line with a cue ball about half way up the table, by the side pocket, on the other side of the table. You are about three and a half or four and a half feet from the object ball. Now by hitting it a little harder, you can slide the cue ball all the way down to the object ball and make it stop.

You will observe that you have to hit it harder than you would like to and also if there is any error in your shot, either forward, backward, or sideways, that error is **magnified** by the extra force you had to put on it to get it there, not spinning or rolling, but sliding all the way.

Our purpose of this shot is to get there slower, which lowers our error magnitude, but with no spin. I call it "Relaxed Draw". Go back to the strokes we just used to hit the stripes down the table.

Now all we have to do is to time that cue ball, "Slide Area" so it happens just about right before our cue ball hits our target ball.

We hit this stroke lower and slower and "Nice". It is very artistic looking when you find the right speed and follow through. Use a stripe for a cue ball so you may see the action change during the last part of a second, just before the cue ball impacts with the object ball.

Needless to say, you will have to practice these a lot. (We also use this stroke for other shots). **You will be reinforcing the feel of this shot for the rest of your life!!!**

NINETY-MILES PER HOUR

Did I say, "Other shots"? Years ago, a Minnesota State Champion, Eight Ball Team member of mine, (Double Jump Oglesbee), stopped me cold.

He said, "Damn it Doc, how can you hit a long straight in shot at ninety miles an hour, and the cue ball rolls six to ten inches and dies"?

I took a deep breath, now that I knew he wasn't mad at me. This is a big guy.

I explained the relaxed draw phenomenon to him. It seems strange at first that you have to hit the cue ball slightly harder to get it to stop sooner.

That is the way it works, as you have to hit the cue ball harder, to get it to slide or draw and that allows the energy to be absorbed into the object ball, and then the cue ball will move whatever small amount forward or backward, depending on how much draw or slide or "Let up", you used. You are controlling the cue ball to have a small amount of spin at the impact area, with the object ball. Whew!! Sit down. I'm slow.

By using a variation on the relaxed draw you may manipulate the cue balls roll distance, action at a distant point, after striking an object ball.

This is going to take a L-O-T of practice, but the raw power gained, makes it worthwhile. Yeah, you guessed it. You have to FEEL it.

Line up a long straight in with the target ball about in the middle of the table. You may start with a draw or a slide shot. You will end up using them both.

While shooting the target ball into or towards the far corner pocket, and using a stripe for the cue ball, (it helps you see the action), slide the cue ball so that it starts to roll just a few inches in front of your target ball.

However many inches in front of the target ball, the cue ball starts to roll, it will roll about the same distance past where you hit the target ball. If the two balls are farther apart, instead of sliding the cue ball, you may have to use some draw and relax it, to get the desired effect.

Depending on the distance between the two balls, you will have to judge the cue ball speed/spin by practicing forever!!!

I mentioned "Feel Shot". This is really a Feel Shot, as you will have to practice these for the rest of your life, even when you understand them.

Are you starting to feel as artistic as Beethoven yet? (Small inside joke, a player buddy of mine thought Beethoven was an oil painter artist).

Most players just roll the ball where ever on this type of shot. Once you semi-master it, you will have some control. Yes, you have to hit the shot harder than normal to get it to stop sooner. You can also use a little bit more spin to get it to back up, but that is just a draw shot and you probably knew that. (this is what STROKE is all about)

There are players all over this country that have no idea that this shot effect is possible.

Relaxed draw to control forward roll, who'd-a-Thunk-it? Are we having fun yet?

I hope you are beginning to see the power this adds to your game, by learning to control the cue ball at a distant point. This is both artistically and emotionally satisfying. You are learning to bend the cue balls action to your will. You will gradually learn from both the good and bad strokes. At first you will be inconsistent, look to your self.

Every variation in the cue balls behavior may be traced back to something you did or didn't do. You can argue with your cue ball if you want, but remember, "The Cue Ball Can't Lie". Are you beginning to realize why a locked stance is required?

The term, relaxed draw now makes sense. You are hitting a draw stroke, but relaxing that stroke to get the speed and spin that you want at a distant point.

See the "Bohemian Curse of Knowledge", later in the text.

FUN WITH RELAXED DRAW AND SOME OTHER STUFF

There are further applications of this phenomenon called "Relaxed Draw". During every cut shot, the amount of forward spin, no spin, or backward spin helps determine the exact exit path of the cue ball off the face, or contact point, of the object ball.

Every shot you shoot, the cue ball's exiting path from the collision point, with the object ball is determined by how much high, or low or no spin is on that cue ball, RIGHT THEN, when the balls hit each other.

It is obvious by now that this whole Dead ball, Sliding ball, and Relaxed Draw, phenomenon requires you to practice with a serious attitude. Isn't it wonderful? It is going to be work, but work that you will enjoy. There is definitely light at the end of the tunnel, and you can see it from here!! You will actually be teaching yourself.

Your thoughts, "If I do this, the cue ball should go there". Did it? If not, why not, try it again. Induce a variable that makes sense to you, and then try it again.

Don't lie to your self. If Mel is not right, you are probably the cause. Is your body locked? Are you hitting "Nice"? Are you stroking level? Remember, Mel should be half way to the target ball before he realizes he has been hit. Are we still having fun, or is it looking more like work?

You have to accept that inconsistent results are due to inconsistent inputs from YOU. The cue ball is incapable of LYING. If your form and function is right so will the cue ball's action be right.

MORE DEAD BALL STUFF

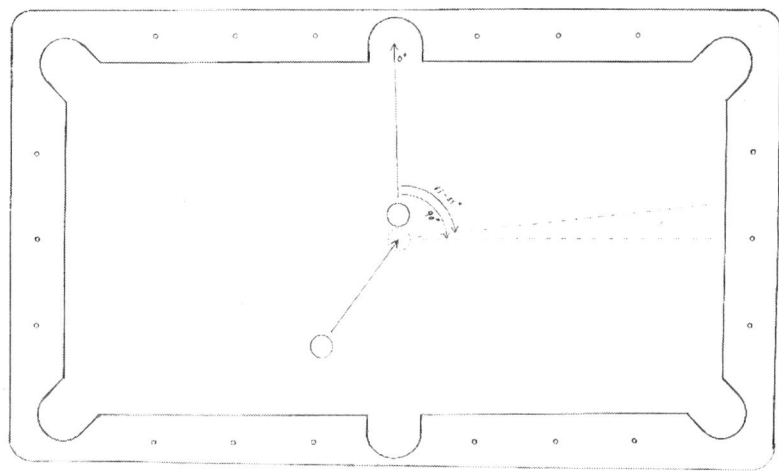

Object ball into side pocket showing cue ball going
off at 83/85 degrees to the end rail

If the cue ball hits the object ball with, "Zero" English, it will kiss off at about 83 to 85 degrees, something just under 90 degrees. It is like a kiss shot with inertia added to the cue ball.

Paul A. "Doc" Rutter

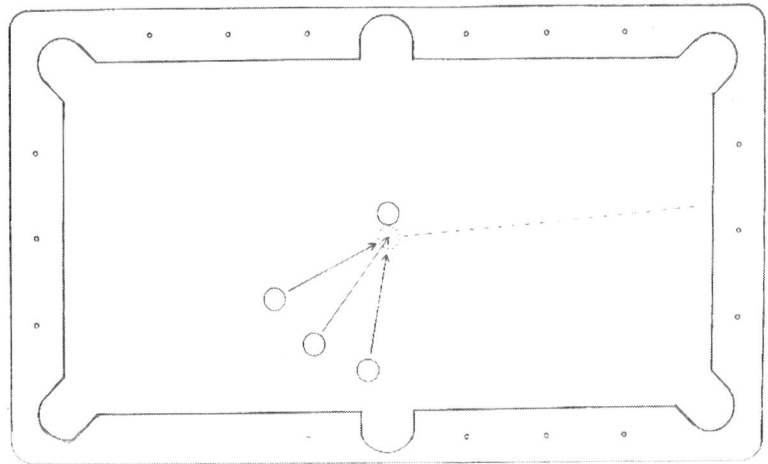

3-cue balls going to same place after hitting ball

Set up the table like the above illustration

You can use any balls as pretend cue balls. The first ball should hit about 90% of the target (object) ball. Middle cue ball should hit about 70% of the target ball, and the last cue ball should hit about 50% of the target ball. By varying the amount of kinetic energy we absorb, we can prove our results.

Stripes as cue balls are more artistically dramatic. Now with a "body lock" stance firmly slide (shoot) each cue ball, one at a time. You will observe that the cue balls, first, do not go to the center diamond, as you may have expected.

Due to "Inertia" they will glance of the object ball at about 83 to 85 degrees from the object ball's path to the side pocket.

This is a fact, Jack!! Even though the cue balls come into the impact area from different angle, if they arrive with NO SPIN, they will all three kiss off to the same exit path. If your cue balls don't go to the same spot, sorry pal, it is your inconsistency.

Check your consistency of stance, stroke, speed, cue tip height, etc. Now this is a rock that you can carry around and throw at your opponents any time you need to.

Try any cut shot on the table and you have an absolute starting point path for your cue ball.

Now I give you the reality news. What if you don't want to go there? That is not really so bad. Do you want to go forward of that path? Apply some high English. Do you want to go backwards from that path? Apply some draw. Your individual style, stroke, cue chalk, etc. will be yours. As long as you can get consistent results, Work it Henry!!

If one of your friends gets slightly different results it is not fatal. He may not be hitting the exact same spots as you are. As long as you can control what you do to your own satisfaction you are playing your game, to your style

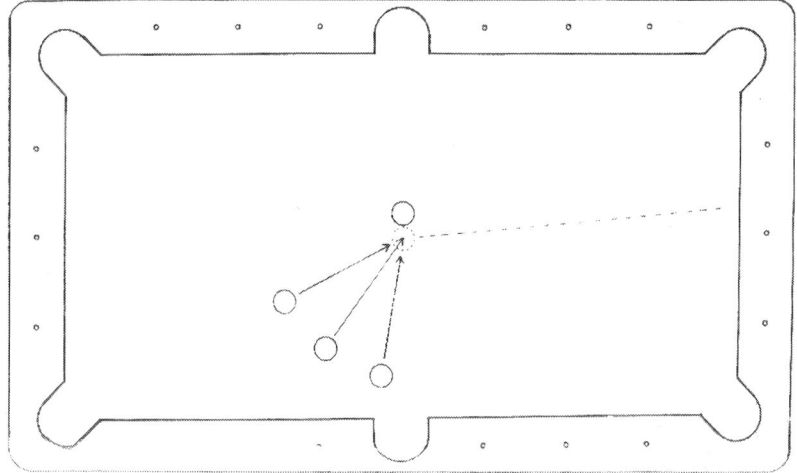

Same 3 cue balls, different explanation

I will use this same illustration, but now I am going to apply high and low spin to the cue ball.

ADDING SPIN

Set up the shot as illustrated don't worry about getting it perfect. This works all over. An object ball is set up one ball width from the center of the table.

Find the center by lining your cue stick with the diamonds and then setting the ball next to it. Chalk spin, mark, that spot. A cue ball frozen to that object ball should end up in the middle of the table and that gives us a practice reference point exactly in the middle of the table.

If you struck that cue ball that we just froze to our object ball with a third ball, it would kiss off and go down to the head rail hitting on the center diamond, 90 degrees from the path of the object ball, that path, into the pocket, is designated zero degrees, You can prove this if you want, by shooting it once.

With reference to the above illustration, set up three cue balls, like in that picture.

As soon as you start applying spin to the cue ball, the resulting exit paths change. Let us use ten miles per hour as an arbitrary power value if you are starting with the 50% cue ball, you will only be expending five miles an hour of our power. When you hit the target ball, with five miles per hour of kinetic energy left, in the sliding cue ball, our spin can have very little effect. Three to five degrees variance of the cue balls exit path from the "NO SPIN" path is my guess.

If we shoot the 70% cue ball we get more variance due to more kinetic energy, seven miles per hour, is absorbed into our target ball. With only three miles per hour of energy left in the cue ball, our spin has more power, relatively, but can still only influence the exit path by about another ten degrees.

When we get to the 90% cue ball, now there is only 10% of the kinetic power left in the cue ball, after collision and the spin now can vary the exit path by about forty five, or so, degrees. This action is not linear and changes drastically as you approach a straight in shot.

One summation I like is, "If you play for straight in, or near straight in shots, you will have much more spin control over your cue ball exit paths, from the impact point with the object ball. This works well with pattern play, which I will explain later.

LEARN BY WATCHING, NOW

Now, I have a scoop for you. Once you have semi-mastered this concept, you can watch the poolroom bully and he can no longer hide his secrets from you. You will be able to observe. On any shot, where his cue ball goes, (on the exit path), but now you will know what spin he had to have had on the cue ball to make it go there. There are three normal cue ball actions, a Sliding cue ball, a Rolling cue ball and a Spinning cue ball. Each will give different cue ball exit paths from the object ball.

I can watch a player's cue ball action for a game or two and I have a very good idea of whether he will be difficult to play or not.

SOME CUE BALL MAGIC

The cue ball, if it could think, thinks that the object ball it hits is a Flat Wall, and it glances off accordingly. Well Cashmere, the look on your face says, that you have some doubts.

Think about it. I have previously explained how a cue ball, arriving with "NO" English will glance off at about 83 to 85 degrees? This is a very powerful tool.

Imagine a target ball setting in the jaws, centered in a corner pocket, at the foot of the table. Now put the cue ball on the foot spot.

Shoot the cue ball firmly, causing it to slide, with no spin, into the target ball. Since the target ball is in the jaws of the pocket, we have a large error angle to work with. Start on one side of the object ball and slowly, shot after shot work your way across the face of that target ball. Keep changing the hit point on the object ball by one or two degrees, each time you shoot.

Use a medium hard stroke, as you want to insure, that the cue ball arrives with No Spin. Surprise, surprise, look at all the different exiting paths for your cue ball. That is pure physics, and under your control, with absolutely NO ENGLISH.

I have seen good players, with a ball deep in the pocket, so uncertain of where they can make the cue ball go, that they end up drawing off of the face of the object ball, as if they were afraid to shoot it any other way.

Yes, it is some more practicing for you, and you will never be afraid of this one again.

The next variation is to introduce sidespin, as the rails are close and you will get a definite response, but you can also play with that, only after you learn the "no spin" shots first. Here again, you are your own teacher. The more you experiment, the stronger your game becomes.

BODY LOCK STANCE

Books you may have read will spend pages and pictures on proper stance. Once you figure out what you are trying to accomplish, stance is somewhat common sense.

I had to cover some of the previous information, so you would understand how important your stance is.

<u>YOU MUST SHOOT FROM A BODY LOCKED POSITION.</u>

Nothing should move on your body except your shooting arm, from the shoulder down. You must be comfortable enough to thrust the cue stick forward about 8 to 16 inches. (Don't beat me up, this is an estimate, your stroke is your own).

Don't get mired down in Forearm and Shoulder, microscopic differences. Some trial and error will show you what stroke works for what you are trying to do.

Some players will have a long distance between their cue ball and their bridge hand so they can accomplish a long back swing. As a pool player you are not hitting a ninety-three miles-per-hour baseball. You may shoot an estimated five to twenty five miles per hour. I haven't specifically measured this.

Break shots have been timed at tournaments, with radar at some where over thirty and under forty miles-per-hour. I believe the record is in the higher thirties.

A normal pool shot requires a short, or very little, backstroke, but a long follow through, depending on what you are trying to do. Your bridge should be locked in concrete.

Your rear handgrip has to be variable. It has to be tight enough to get the cue moving and then loosening up to get what ever wrist action you need for the current shot.

There is no absolute here. That rear handgrip is a "human" thing. The grip is, (are you ready for this?), more of a "Feel" thing.

On a short punch stop stroke you may grip the cue stick tightly, as you don't want excessive speed or spin.

A long relaxed draw may need the extra action of a good wrist snap, for that little extra spin. The grip is totally your call. The old cliché, "Different Strokes For Different Folks", definitely applies here.

More experimenting is required on your part. These variations of grip need practice, so that you can control the input affect to get the resulting effect.

Take your normal, bayonet fighter's stance. Spread your feet about shoulder's width, a little wider can't hurt. With your bridge side foot forward and your cue butt side foot a little rearward, back under the cue stick's butt, you should feel comfortable and not on any strain at all. Now line up on a cue ball. With your body locked, now flex your knees. Notice the cue tip is traveling up and down in an alarming fashion. Probably more than you would expect. Any body movement during the execution of the shot will affect the cue tip's height at the cue ball.

This is why I advise playing with a shorter bridge. The shorter the distance is from your bridge to the cue ball, the less addressing error will be with any inadvertent body movement.

Many players do not hit the cue ball exactly where they are aiming, due to poor body lock and/or stance. If you point that out to them, be prepared to hear a whole lot of "Who Shot John" rationalization. When they get inconsistent results, they lose confidence in their play due to this inconsistency. They don't have a clue as to why they didn't get the result that they planned. Generally a short backstroke coupled with a longer follow through consistently gets the job done. This allows you to hit the balls softer and get more action. I learned this from watching the Professional players.

By minimizing the bridge to cue ball distance, you minimize any body movement error. This is free and cannot hurt you.

NATURAL SLIP STROKE

At the end of the stroke, some players actually let the cue stick slide forward by loosening their rear handgrip, as a continuation of that stroke. This slide varies and is about three to six or even eight inches. This is what is called a natural slip stroke.

Try some practice draw shots using a slip stroke. You may really like the results. The slip stroke adds some speed and spin, but not in a measurable quantity.

There is a consistency factor here, as the slip stroke hits the ball with only the weight of the cue stick, not your arm muscles and the cue stick together.

If I am playing straight pool, as I progress into a rhythm, I have a tendency to slip stroke more and more as I like that constant weight feeling of the cue stick hitting the cue ball.

This is only mentioned for your info and is not something I am trying to talk you into. It is something you may want to experiment with. What could it hurt?

Some players don't like it at all, and would question your sanity if you try to describe it to them. Try it. If you like it or not, it is your choice.

JACKED UP CUE STICK

A jacked up cue is a trap of ignorance. Being ignorant doesn't mean you are dumb. It means you lack that experience or information in that particular situation.

The PLANE of your English application is the same as the PLANE of your cue stick. That is why we try to ALWAYS try to keep the cue stick as level with the table's surface as is practical.

If you have to jack up your cue, to shoot a certain shot, never apply, even a little bit of side English. If you apply any side English at all, you are effectively shooting a "Masse".

Hitting the cue ball down the center is okay; anything else and your cue ball will curve some unspecified amount, on the way to the target ball!!

A jacked up cue, on the break, is what causes the cue ball to fly off of the table. Always try to keep your cue stick level, near to the same plane as the table that the balls are on.

Always approach a jacked up shot with fear and respect and after a successful stroke, wipe your sweating brow and exclaim, "Whew, that was close". Then, theatrics aside, your SWEATERS are entertained; now get back to running out, ha.

Yes, I know. What is MASSE? Our wonderful billiard clown Rudolph Wanderone, AKA, "Minnesota Fats", when asked, stated, "Masse is French for, hard shot".

Fats couldn't even spell Minnesota, and "Borrowed" the name after the movie, "The Hustler" was released in 1961.

Fatty was always fun and the players liked his outrageous, "true life tales", that mostly could not be verified. He was also a better than average One-Pocket player.

MASSE

This is going to confuse you. A masse shot is exactly like a relaxed draw shot with the cue stick jacked up at an elevated angle in relation with the Plane of the pool table, and some degree of side English.

You have an obstructing ball that you want to curve around. You have to shoot to an imaginary spot past the obstructing ball and let the kinetic energy wear out, by sliding on the cloth and when that kinetic energy wears out, the spin, (exaggerated high or low on the side you are trying to curve to) will now allow the spin to twist the cue ball in a curving manner back toward the ball you are trying to hit.

Let us get back to that English. If you are curving to the right, you must hit the cue ball with high (2:30) or low (4:30) right hand English. Both high and low will work, but to different degrees. Your cue must be elevated to about 15 or 20 degrees.

The high will be more exaggerated, but the low is more controllable. The high English can also be increased, by raising the cue stick higher and higher. With the low English you don't have quite as much range of cue stick elevation.

I use the low English as much as I can, especially on a longer masse, as it gives me a more controlled longer curve.

I use the higher elevated cue stick and high side English if the shot is short with a more exaggerated curve required.

Exaggerated "trick shot" masse shots are not very practical but if you insist, try a few. I hope you don't damage anything.

I hate to tell you this, but yes, you will have to practice these to get the "Feel" of how they work. These are not easy, but if you have a good feel for your variable distance relaxed draw shots that will help you feel these masse shots.

MORE BALLS AND CLOTH INFO

Never, *Never*, <u>Never</u> use side English unless you know exactly why you are using it. Sidespin does not change the path of the cue ball off the face of an object ball. It will give you visible action once the cue ball hits a rail though.

To change the path of a cue ball off the object ball, use high or low spin . . . **(Period)**

Sidespin has almost no effect, on the cue ball. Thousands of players routinely add sidespin to every shot thinking that they are adding direction to the cue ball. It doesn't happen. More often than not, (*wait for it*),—"It is more trouble than it is worth".

*Used properly, sidespin can be a useful too*l. Many players use excessive sidespin without ever making the effort to find out what it is costing them.

Oh, *Save the Baby*, is he is going to talk about squirt and deflection? Yes He Is, being an, ahem, older, more experienced player.

Back in the 40's, 50's 60's, the terms Squirt and deflection were unknown. Clay balls, coupled with Mali, Stevens, and House cloth that were all at about a twenty-ounce weight and gave the balls and cloth a consistent friction relationship. Both the cloth and the balls had more friction than the newer, so called, better equipment that came later.

In the late 50's & early 60's, Cast Phenolic balls came into more common use. Luther (Wimpy) Lassiter exclaimed, about the new balls, "These damn balls slide like a glass ash tray". (I will explain, to the younger players, what an ashtray is later). Wimpy was right. The new balls had less friction on the bottom where they rubbed against the cloth. This equipment change also brought out the dreaded "Skid" effect that we have all been bitten with. A skid is when a target ball, instead of going toward the pocket when hit, slides slightly sideways, in the direction of the incoming cue ball's path, for a short distance. This effect has been blamed on unidentified dirt or chalk clumps on the surface of one of the involved balls. I don't know if it has ever been proven, but I know I get upset when it happens as it usually costs me a game or match. The skid seems to occur when a **dead or sliding** cue ball is used and the two balls are about six to, not more than, twenty inches apart, with a softer or medium stroke.

If the balls are farther apart some forward roll on the cue ball seems to be an automatic antidote. Any small amount of spin may be applied, but we never can anticipate when it is going to occur. **The Object ball doesn't skid if the cue ball is spinning!!!**

Adjustments had to be made, by the great players, the rest just muddled along. From this beginning period, players gradually got used to the new Phenolic balls and all was well until the movie, "The Color of Money" came along in 1987,

All Hell broke loose. The billiard world, all at once became filled with new, self-styled, experts and they all wanted to be the best, so they could attract the most customers.

Simonis cloth had been around for years, but due to price was only used sparingly. Now the new experts, with the, "we are doing it better attitude", started using Simonis 760 and/ or the equivalent in Granito cloths.

These were significantly faster cloths and all the new nine ballers loved it. This love appeared to come from a combination of, if the balls go farther, I may get lucky, and since I don't know how to play position anyway, I couldn't care less, ha.

Common sense soon kicked in and most rooms backed up slightly to the 860-type cloth, which is about 10% less fast. You don't dare to say, "Slower" to a nine-ball player.

The 860 Simonis and the Championship, or Granito equivalent has become pretty much the standard cloths today. These new cloths along with the previously introduce Phenolic balls now have their own, less friction relationship, with each other.

All the new, smarter Cue Makers saw a marketing gizmo and the industry coined the "Squirt & Deflection" phrase.

This phrase took its place in the Billiard media speak and we are stuck with that and the players are stuck with the very real physics facts that spawned it.

Many cue makers are making "Magic" cue stick shafts with special components or lamination. They are all advertised to negate or eliminate this physics factor. You have to be your own judge.

A lot of players don't understand the, squirt & deflection concept well enough to benefit from the new "Magic" shafts. They will learn in time, OR NOT.

All cue shafts deflect, some more, some less.

This new less friction situation means that if you load up your cue ball with lot of side English, the cue ball, when struck, will not just go 100% straightforward. You are hitting a sphere, on its side. Due to less friction between the cloth and the bottom of the ball, the cue ball will jump sideways slightly and then generally proceed to the object ball, and will hit that ball, just to the side a little bit. You guessed it, just enough to miss your shot. This all happens in a split second and you will not be able to see it happen, but you will see the results as a missed shot. See the example in the illustration below.

SQUIRT

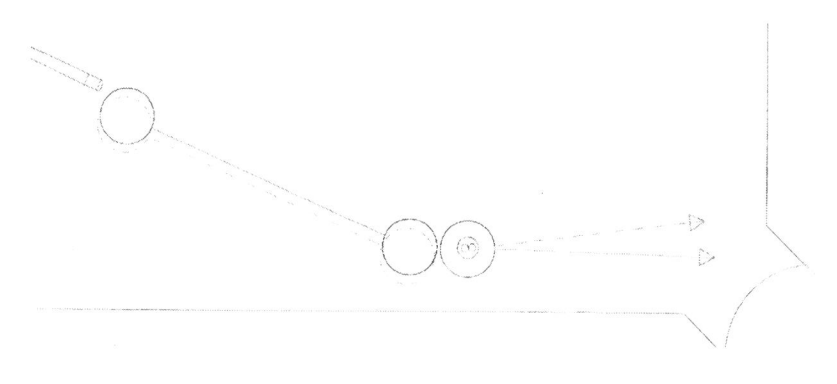

Squirt

If you want to keep on using a lot of side English, you must learn to compensate for this situation, or you can continue to miss shots and wonder why. Compensating is adjusting your aim point to allow for the estimated cue shaft deflection and the resulting squirt of the cue ball during the current shot.

You may also modify your play, with regard to, how much sidespin you apply to the cue ball. Don't reach out so far on the cue ball. This is what the pros do.

Naturally artistic players seem to be able to load up their cue ball with as much English as they want, and "Get Away with It" I guess that is why we call them artistic players. Their subconscious mind automatically does the adjusting for them. The rest of us have to work to find the compromise point.

Here is a band-aid for you. You need to practice this, so you can convince both sides of your brain that you know what is "happening". Line up a simple, half ball shot, cutting the target ball to the right. Load up the cue ball with as much sidespin to the right as you care to use. Try about 2:30 on the clock face. Shoot and observe the shot. We don't care about the object ball aim it into the pocket. Note where you hit the rail, with the cue ball, and the amount of the deflect angle caused by the sidespin. Now shoot it the same way, but instead of hitting the cue at 2:30, hit the cue ball at about 1:00.

You will be surprised to find out that the cue ball will go about the same place and rebound off the rail at a similar angle, as the previous shot. It may not be exactly the same, but close enough when you consider that you don't have that big exaggerated squirt error.

Each player has to prove this to himself, as the emotional side of your brain will say, "No way Jose". Yes, way, and you can do it over and over until you have proven to yourself that you don't need as much English applied, to the cue ball, to do about the same job. Convince your self. Individual results may vary.

Cause and effect, as you affect the application of the English on the cue ball, you change the effect of the results. You are once again teaching yourself how to play.

Really try hitting the ball closer to the centerline. You will see surprising results.

The Barefoot Cue Ball

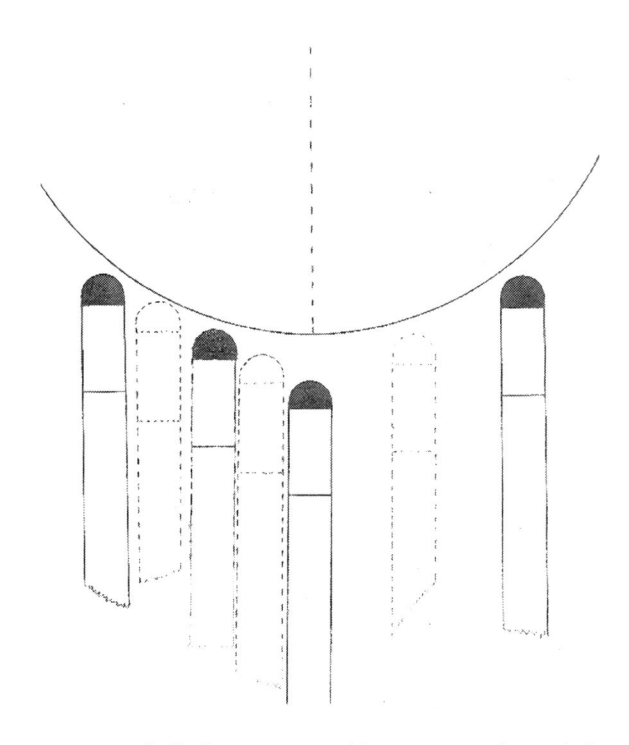

Large cue ball showing several hit points, side English

When you take the time to prove these simple physics concepts, you will gain miles of good results that are cemented into your brain for the rest of your billiards-playing career. You will also be able to deal with changes.

BOHEMIAN-GYPSY CURSE OF KNOWLEDGE

You can no longer pretend that you don't know how or why something occurred.

If you are playing on different cloth or older, clay balls, you can now adjust accordingly. This will probably never come up.

If something new comes up, you are better prepared to make adjustments and deal with it. Once you know the physics of the cue ball, you cannot pretend you don't. There will be a spot back in your brain that will call you a liar. Get out there and do the **work.**

Some players will listen to this information and since it makes sense to them, they don't bother to practice any of it, and never develop the FEEL of the various strokes.

PRACTICE

Well-executed practice is the training of your subconscious mind. The logical/functional side of your brain has to show the emotional/artistic side of your brain that you know what the heck you are doing. This builds confidence.

If you can get both sides of your brain to agree with each other, you will eliminate the "Choking Up" syndrome. The emotional side of your brain is the one that screams, "Wait, Stop, Don't, Shift, Falter, etc.

The local loser in the bar, as he is paying you off, states, "You sure are a lucky player". And your reply, "yes, I am, and the more I practice the luckier I get". (An old sports competition joke)

Valuable practice is where you set up a shot with consistent conditions, and only one or two variables. By controlling the set conditions, you create a logical thought process. Any changes in your input, allows or causes the change in your result.

Every player, sooner or later starts playing 8 ball with himself, and he thinks he is practicing. Not so, Herschel. You are only reinforcing any habit you already have, good or bad, and you are not learning anything new.

Sorry to burst your bubble. The, so-called, practicing player continues through the rack changing side after every missed shot until he has cleared the table.

What did he learn? Nothing new, that's for sure. He just reinforced his mediocrity. Any mistakes or bad form or wrong thinking has just been reinforced in that player's sub-conscious mind.

If you insist on playing eight ball alone, use a different strategy. Break, pick a side, and run as far as you can. If you fail, stop and analyze, why did you fail? What could you have done differently? Re-rack, and start again.

Every time you fail, start over. It is more work, but it raises the priority of why you are there.

Let me give you a simple, better idea. This is just one example. Using-a-chalk-mark spin, mark a target ball spot at the foot half's middle side diamond, one diamond out from the side rail. Use the end rail for this reference. Mark the cue ball by the side pocket the same distance from the side rail. (See Illustration below) Any similar shot will do. Now you are controlling the starting spots for both balls. The pocket isn't going anywhere, so it is also controlled. This set up also controllers the exact kiss angle of the cue ball off the face of the target ball. Shoot into the corner pocket continuously.

Start with a dead sliding cue ball to establish a starting point then go to the top of the cue ball and on each shot lower your cue tip about one half of a tip. Continue to the bottom of the ball. What did you see? Where you surprised?

This is just like the Spray Shot, only starting from different spots. Do it again. Psst, watch it, you are actually learning some thing. Scary isn't it.

Every time you change your input English. You get a different output result. Your sub-conscious mind is recording all of this. Change the conditions of your shot, move to different spots, but keep the same positive attitude. When your mind leaps ahead and asks, what if I do this? What if I do that? You don't need me. Set a shot up and prove to yourself what the results are. You just answered your own question. That's what I did!!

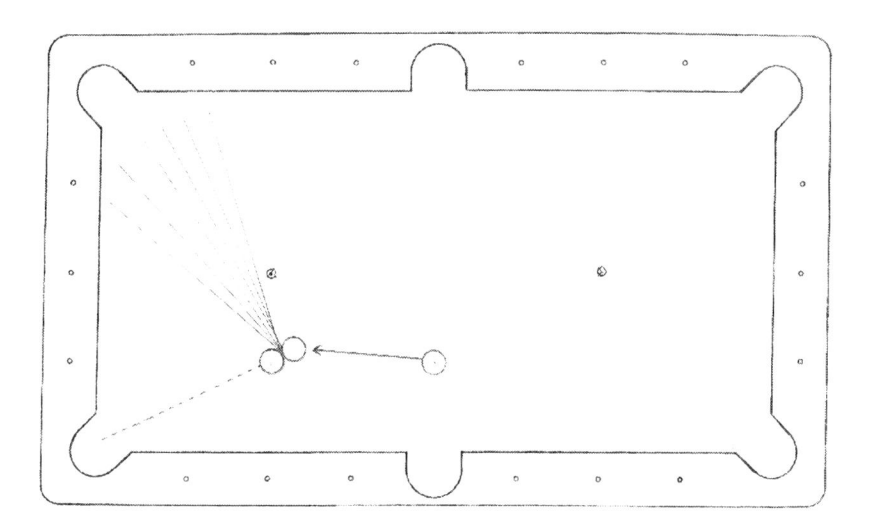

This is just like the earlier spray shot, but in a different direction, and different angle. Start at the top of the cue ball and slowly work

your way down. Watch the exit path of the cue ball change. Stroke each shot with enough force to arrive with the spin applied. A soft stroke will just roll the ball.

PRACTICE DRILLS

Grow your own!! Just like the one in the above illustration. Practice drills make good instruction book page fillers. Shooting a shot or a series of shots over and over will cause you to get very good at those shots. Then you may hope they come up in a game once in a while. Usually they don't show up. Based on what you are reading here, you can come up with your own practice shots. Use the "Spin Chalk" marking method.

You can shoot as many of any shot you care to practice. What are you doing? You already know how to pocket the ball. Work on the position play.

That is not what you are practicing. You must practice good form throughout all practice shots. Start with Body Lock, stance, and bridge; follow through, speed of stroke, grip, wrist action, etc. Now by changing your degree of high and low spin on the cue ball, you can observe the various exit paths, from the object ball's contact point.

If I do this, what happens? If I do that, what happens? Why did it go there? What if I change English?

Shoot each one several times to establish your consistency. What are your inputs? What are your results?

You will soon get used to this method, and will enjoy being able to teach yourself some of the things you may have been asking your acquaintances about. When you ask those questions, most players feel obligated to give you an answer, of various values, as very few have the guts to say, "I don't Know", and if they are stumped, they will usually make something up.

AROUND THE ENGLISH CLOCK

Set up a shot as in the illustration below. Apply English to the cue ball, starting at 12 Noon. Shoot three or four shots with that spin applied and observe the cue ball's exit path. Now go to one o'clock, shoot three or four shots, then two o'clock, etc. Work your way around the cue ball clock. You will be surprised that some different spins appear to give similar results. Learn from it.

Learning where you can make the cue ball go, from a "frozen to the rail" shot, will allow you to break out ball clusters easier, from all over the table.

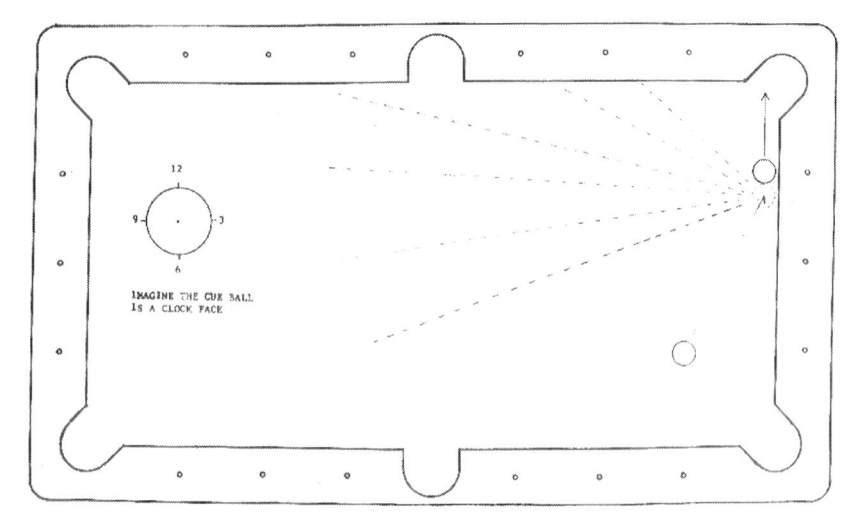

Around the clock practice shot

JUMPING THE CUE BALL

This phenomenon came about with the cast Phenolic balls. The clay ball would not jump by hitting down on them, as they didn't compress. For years it was illegal to jump a ball by scooping under the cue ball and nothing else worked. When the phenolic balls came on the scene slowly players learned, mostly by accident, that if you elevate your cue stick and shoot with quick acceleration, the cue ball would jump. Why? The phenolic resin is resilient and compresses slightly when impacted. This resiliency causes a slight basketball effect. Squash the cue ball into the pool table by driving it downwards and it rebounds proportionally. If hit with enough force it will bounce a surprising amount.

The Barefoot Cue Ball

Early in the jumping days Sammy Jones could set a cue ball one-chalk width away from an object ball and jump that full ball using only a cue shaft.

Earl Strickland shocked a TV audience by jumping a full ball with a full-length cue stick on National TV.

The short jump cues are light and they are easier to accelerate. The higher the cue stick speed the higher/longer the cue ball will jump. Snappy wrist action enhances this Activity. There are other semi-secret features needed, but I won't reveal them here, as they are constantly evolving. **A dart stroke seems to work best.**

SPINS AND THROWS

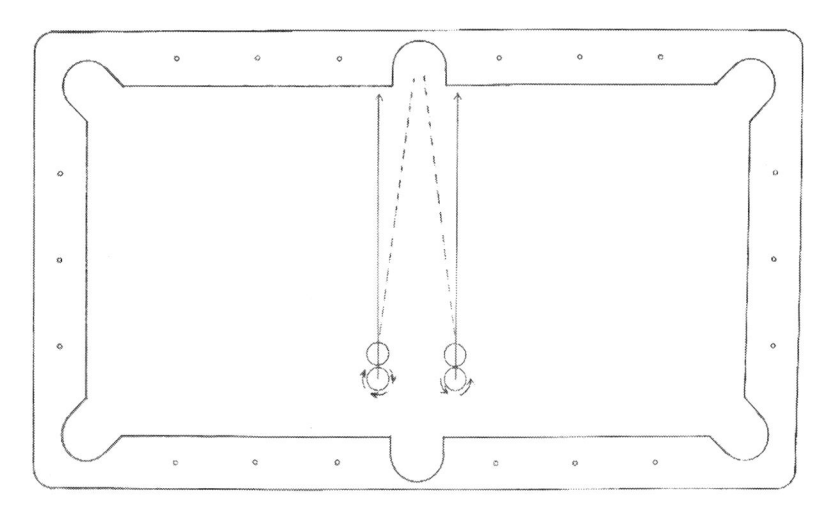

Spins and throws

Most current "How To" books get this info right, but do they explain it to your satisfaction? Sit down on the other side of the table and scoot up to the side pocket. I promise I won't jump cue balls at you. (Some times I lie). Let me dazzle you with fancy words and Magical shots, ha. Did you buy Bob Byrne's book? Get it out now and follow me along.

In the normal coarse of play, once in a while, your cue ball will freeze up against one of your target balls. Wherever they are aimed, they are aimed.

If they happen to line up, aimed at a pocket, good for you. Shoot your cue ball slightly to one side, about one or two degrees, to avoid a follow scratch.

Some times it is necessary to elevate your cue stick, to avoid a double hit foul. Do not use any sidespin, when the balls are lined up on the pocket.

If the frozen balls line up slightly to one side of the pocket, they may be "Thrown" in by using a little physics magic. Due to the friction factor between two balls, the direction and spin of the cue ball can and will drag the target ball slightly to one side.

Determine which way you need to throw the object ball and then apply the opposite spin to the cue ball. Just remember, to throw left, spin right. To throw right, spin left.

Always check your local league or tournament rule, for push throw rules.

The spin on the cue ball rubs against the object ball and drags it slightly off of the aimed line, just enough to make the shot. All the poolroom variables apply. Your stroke, cue tip, chalk, humidity, how clean or dirty the balls are, etc.

Be aware of the variable conditions and in your warm up shots, try two or three throw shots to see, "How are they throwing, today".

You must practice these shots enough, so that they become second nature. Don't let me catch you standing by a pool table, making spinning hand gestures, trying to figure this out, at the point of the shot. Meanwhile your opponent's team smirks and giggles at you.

The next step is a surprise for some. No matter how far the balls are apart, yes, not frozen, a similar action takes place, but to a slightly different degree. Shoot several soft shots, with good follow through, using sidespin and watch those balls turn slight, as they are hit toward the pocket. Every time you hit a ball with sidespin, you run the risk of turning the ball slightly.

Harder shots will diminish the friction and somewhat negate this effect. A softer stroke will enhance it.

You really need to practice these, as they are inconsistent, and vary from day to day. This is why I warn you; don't use excessive sidespin unless you really know what you are doing.

The inherent surface friction between the balls allows this phenomenon to occur. Dirty balls usually throw better?

If the attendants at your pool facility polish the balls, they will throw considerably less. You are now warned.

PUSH THROW

This next shot looks like the last shot that I showed you. I mean we start out with two frozen balls. By using the same, friction between balls, information we can accomplish a true push throw. By aiming your cue stick about forty-five degrees to the side, and pointing in the direction that you want to throw the target ball. **Use no sidespin.**

In recent years, some leagues have altered their ruling to fit the amateur referee's inability to call or see this shot correctly, when it occurs.

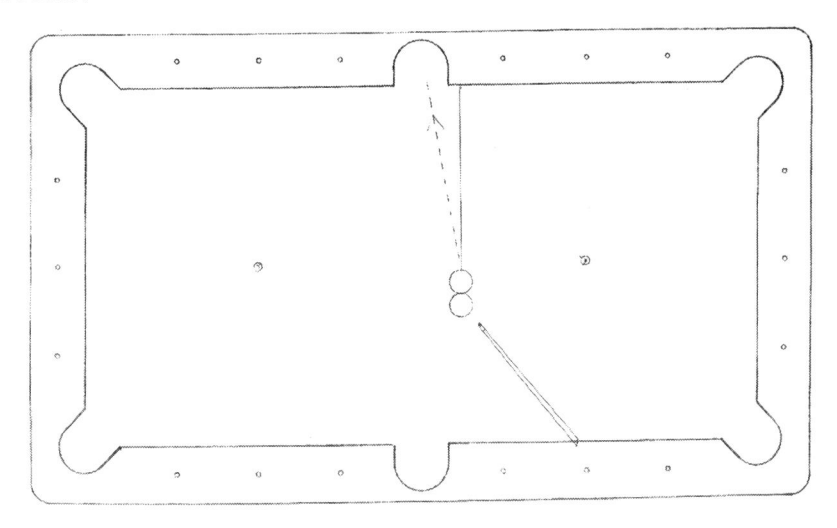

Push throw

In a normal shot, the contact between a cue ball and an object ball is instantaneous and not much odd or unusual takes place. In our proposed test shot, we are actually pushing into the target ball with the cue ball, and for a split second they are held together.

Paul A. "Doc" Rutter

We can slightly "push" that ball, off line and toward our intended pocket. This allows our friction factors to work a little different than a normal shot. Again we drag the target ball off line from its normal path. No sidespin is applied to the cue ball. Use a smooth stroke with good follow through.

If the balls were truly frozen, no double hit foul will occur. Remember to shoot in the direction in which you want to throw the target ball. Practice and experimenting will give you personal power over this situation.

If your two frozen balls happen to be lined up, straight into the pocket, elevate your cue about forty five degrees and stroke it while aiming only about one or two degrees to the side. You don't want to throw a shot off that doesn't need to be thrown. If the balls are frozen, no double hit foul will occur.

DEAD COMBINATIONS

There is no such thing as a dead combination!! Having said that, I must explain. The uninformed player looks at two frozen target balls, that happen to be aimed at a pocket, and he declares, "They are dead, I can't miss". The balls may in fact be "dead", but they can be missed. If you hit the second ball back, on one side or the other, that second ball, as it scoots away, will drag the first ball with it, slightly. So if two balls are lined up, you must still hit the second ball back, on the end that lines up with the pocket. This prevents any unintended throw action.

If you hit the second ball back, on either side, it will throw the first ball off line to the opposite side that you hit.

If the two balls are lined up slightly off-line, hit the second ball back on the opposite side of the intended throw line. The second ball will push the first ball on to the new throw line. Play with this until it becomes second nature.

MULTIPLE BALL THROWS

When you have three or more balls lined up, and the first two are frozen, the third ball back gives direction to the second ball back and the second ball back drags the first one off-line.

The first two balls both have to go in the same direction.

Any balls back of the third one, are just, "power-pass-through-balls", and do not affect the direction of the first, or primary ball.

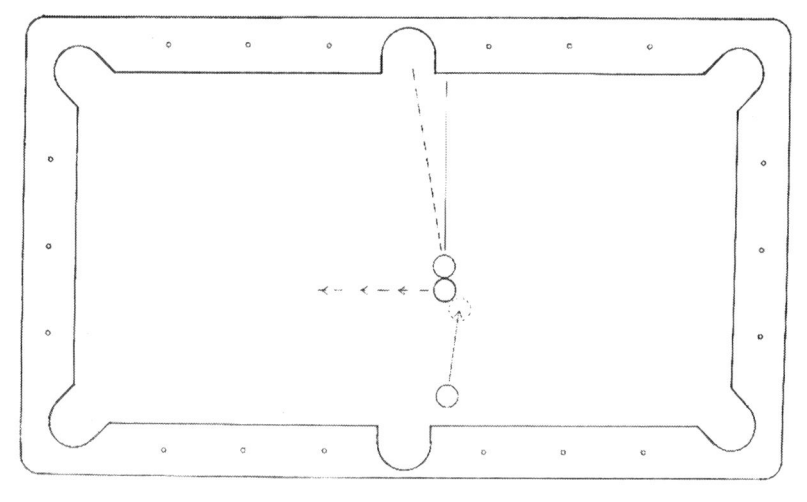

Hit throw

FROZEN KISS SHOTS

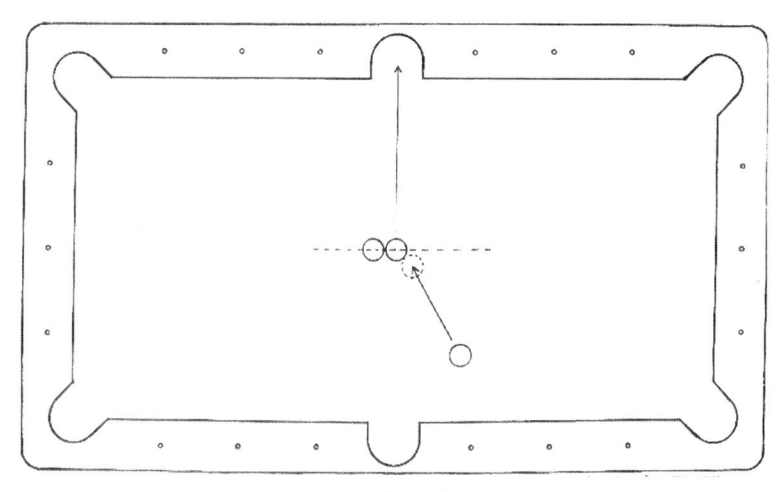

Frozen kiss shot

This is the Icing, on your Small Table 8-ball game, cake. Kiss shots are another game quality, separator in the Talent Pool. Frozen ball kiss shots are simple to analyze and execute, with one exception.

They don't come up much, but if you don't understand them, you will never understand the rest of their impact on your general play.

As a starting point, line up two frozen balls anywhere on the table surface. Draw an imaginary line through the middle of the two balls. If you hit the one closest to the cue ball at about a forty-five degree angle, with high English or no English, that ball will kiss off at a true ninety degrees from our imaginary drawn line. See how easy that is?

Now are you ready for the "Doctors" Bohemian artistic variation? If you dismiss the English applied to the cue ball, you may get in trouble. This is one of those double-edged swords.

If you should inadvertently or deliberately, happen to apply any draw to the cue ball, some, but not all, of this cue ball backspin will transfer to the target ball. Due to friction, this becomes topspin and will cause the struck ball to slightly spin forward, about three to seven degrees, off of your normal target ball's path.

Whoa, major error here. Like the rest of this "Mumbo-Jumbo", it works two ways. We can avoid it and we can also make it work for us.

If our kiss shot is "on" we just hit it with a sliding or rolling cue ball. However, if our kiss path is "Short" of the intended pocket, we may influence it forward by pushing it with a nice smooth draw stroke.

Before you ask, it would seem that you could get the intended ball to back up, by using topspin, which could transfer into back spin on the object ball, and pull that ball backwards.

I have experimented with this concept and, if conditions are perfect, it seems to work once in a while. Usually, depending on the cue ball's incoming angle, the target ball can't back up, as it runs immediately back into the cue ball, which is crowding forward, against the target ball. So any spin energy is blocked, by the cue ball's action.

The attempt to back up the kiss shot is too inconsistent to waste time with. You would have to figure out what exact incoming angle will work and which ones don't. It's a revolting development, Cashmere. Draw works, topspin doesn't.

UNFROZEN KISS SHOTS

Now it gets a little more exciting. On the smaller Valley or Diamond tables, the kiss shot is a very valuable tool, and may get you out of seemingly impossible situations. On the smaller table, a player must be a Master position players and a superior strategist.

Many games are played with a, "Make a ball, break a ball strategy. Good strategists must recognize that when an opportunity comes up, for a kiss shot that is not, frozen or near frozen. The balls can be several inches apart and still be excellent candidates for kissing.

In the example below, I show clearing an opponent's ball out of the way by using an unfrozen kiss shot. Note, See the INERTIA section for more info.

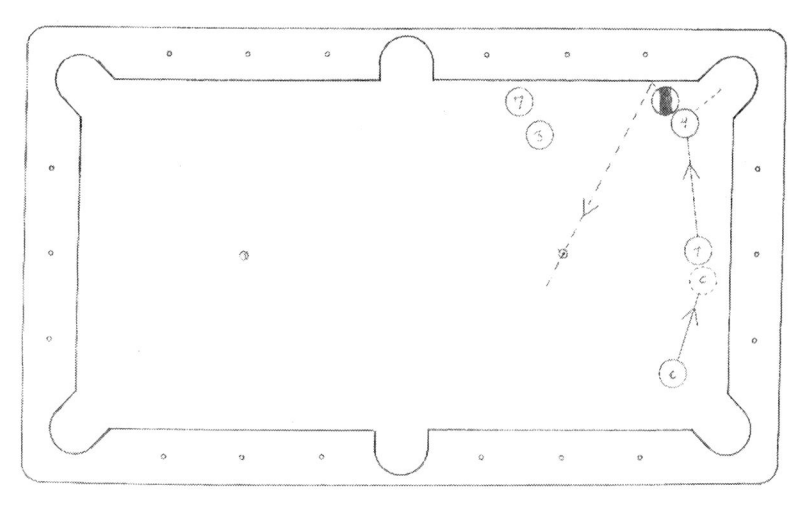

Clearing a pocket with a kiss shot

MY NEMESIS KISS SHOT

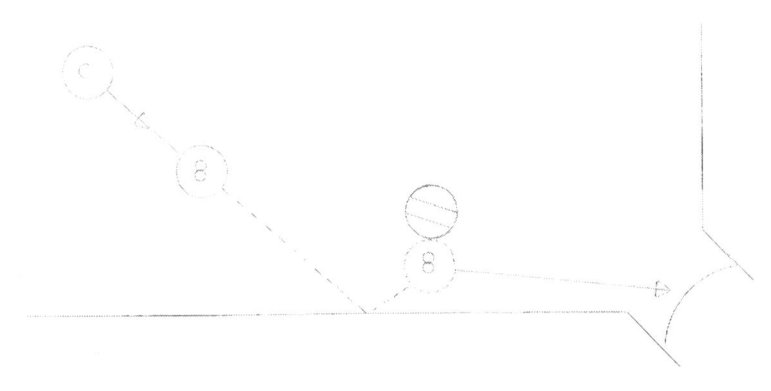

My nemesis shot

Thirty-five years ago, I introduced a kiss shot that I should have kept to myself. Place an opponents object ball by the first diamond of the foot rail, about a ball and a half away from the rail. Place the eight ball in line with the first ball and your target pocket. The pretend situation is, I missed position and ended up on the wrong side of my eight ball, and I am stuck with a losing situation. I now proceed to call the eight ball in the pocket behind the blocking ball. My opponent is eagerly waiting for me to miss. I calmly shoot the eight ball into the foot rail behind the opponents ball, and kiss the eight off of the backside of my opponents ball and into the corner pocket for a very satisfying and surprising miracle win!!

Like throwing a pebble into a still pond, ripples of this shot have come back to haunt me over the years. It is tough to get beat by your own shot.

INERTIA

For unfrozen kiss shots, you have to introduce a new phenomenon called inertia. A player must also not forget about forward, inadvertent cloth roll English. The first struck target ball will arrive at the kiss area, of the second ball, with both inertia and maybe some forward, cloth roll. Get out your mental estimator tools, as we have to make some practical adjustments. You know this is going to require extensive practice.

Look on the bright side. Practice used to be boring. Now you are learning so much and having fun at the same time.

INERTIA means, a body in motion tries to continue that motion. Your kissing ball will try to go in the same direction as it was traveling, even after is kisses off another ball. A ball rolling or sliding that runs into another ball, still tries to continue on its original path, even though it is impossible.

A true ninety-degree kiss cannot occur when speed and direction is applied to the incoming target ball, but it will try.

Blast away at some kiss shots and get your mind around this. Start with a ball close to a pocket a start glancing other balls off of its face, aiming to pocket the incoming, kissing ball off of the inert, kissed ball. You do not have to hit kiss shots hard. If you do hit them hard, you eliminate the inadvertent cloth roll. Other than the cloth roll, the kiss angle is the same regardless of incoming ball's speed. These open tables "Balls Apart" kiss shots take a little more practice work, but you will be paid back, handsomely, over and over with seemingly magic results.

MORE ENERGY MANAGEMENT STUFF

Most players have seen the old trick shot of making two balls jawed one in each of the corner pockets at one end of the table.

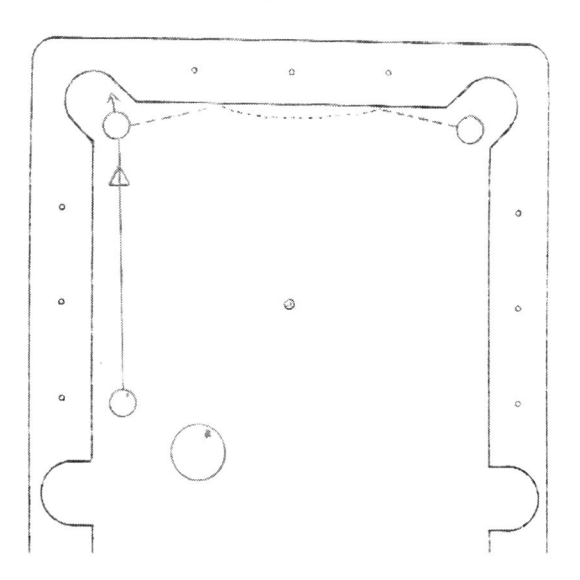

Trick shot, 2 balls in one shot

This is a practical use of energy management to produce a Magic shot. Hit the first ball firmly; almost full face, but slightly on the right side. Use as much top/right spin, about 1:30 or so.

The first target ball absorbs most of the cue balls kinetic energy. Now the cue ball, with almost no kinetic energy remaining glances off the first object ball, and due to the topspin applied, skips gaily along the end rail and pockets the second target ball.

Due to the low kinetic energy and the topspin, the cue ball may hit the end rail more than once, depending on your stroke.

You may have to hit a few of these to get it down. The most important part is that you understand it, and how or why it works.

Why do I show you a trick shot? If you understand this shot you can use both sides of it, good and bad, for your own shot execution.

You have seen players hit a ball down table like this one and have their cue ball die at that end of the table when they really wanted to travel back down to the other end.

If they are questioned, they may reply, "But I used a lot of topspin to make it travel'. Yes, they did, but they absorbed all of their kinetic energy into the first ball and didn't have any gas in the tank to travel any distance.

You, being a smarter player, know that all you have to do is hit the target ball thin, on the side, thereby preserving most of your kinetic energy in the cue ball, to allow it to travel easily down to the other end of the table. You didn't have to hit it hard at all.

Years ago, I had to learn that, "The Hard Way". If you expect to make the cue ball travel any distance, you must leave some kinetic energy in it. Do not expend that energy and expect your cue to go any distance. You remember all this from when I was telling you how to stop the ball. Well this is the other side of the equation.

EIGHT BALL PATTERN SHOOTING

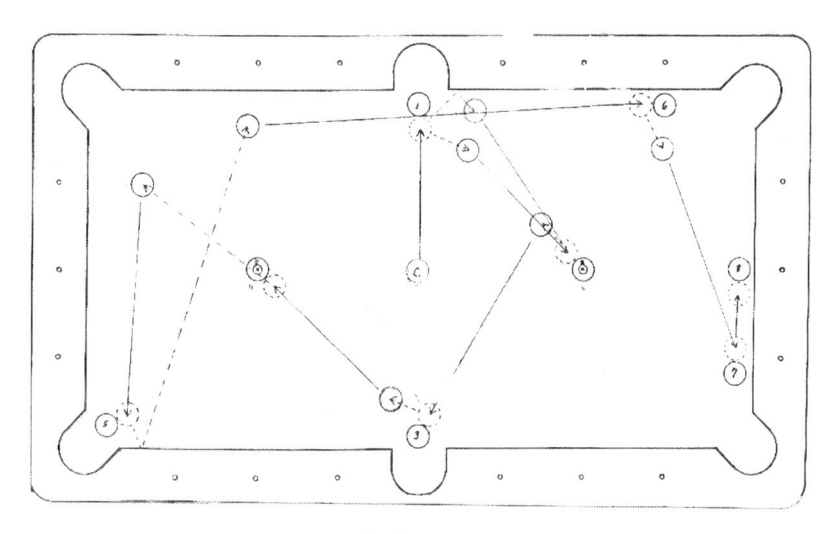

8 ball pattern

Note; place the 1, 3, and 5, balls in the corresponding pocket jaws. Place the 6, 7, 8, One diamond away from pocket about a chalk width off the rail. Place the 2, & 4 balls on the spots. Put Mel in the middle of the table.

I have been using this particular test shot pattern for thirty-five years. Only two or three players have solved it easily. One had been told the semi-secret by a former student. The second one had been a nine-ball player and when question said, "I just shot them in order". The third guy said, "It just made sense to me", he was right.

I wrote this up in one of the first "Billiards Digests" before Mike Pannoza was there. The article included working backwards. It was written in one of the first six issues.

Let us go back to the big picture of the pattern test. Starting backwards from the eight ball. Imagine that you have NO cue ball, and that you have to shoot the eight ball with one of the object balls. The seven-ball is the obvious choice.

So now imagine that, getting back to the real world, with a real cue ball, all I have to do is shoot the seven in such a fashion that the cue ball stays in that immediate area and I should end up with an easy eight ball shot, whew!! Calm down, Elmer there is more of this.

To continue backwards we would shoot the seven from the six's area, and shoot the six from the one's area. You see we have established a four ball out pattern. Shoot the one stop, six stop, seven slight roll, and the eight, stop or slight roll.

Let us slightly change our four-ball out by going backwards to the five-ball instead of the one-ball. The five leads us back to the four, to the three, to the two, and finally the one, which is where we should have started out.

I am not trying to trap anyone, or make a player look foolish. I am trying to prove, to them, how inconsistent they are, when left to their own devices.

Hundreds of players, over thirty-five years failed this simple run out test. They had no concept of pattern play and their resulting failures proved it.

By the way, they all are playing better now, ha. Straight Pool Players eventually learn pattern shooting, almost by accident, if they play long enough.

The big picture is not sweeping or cleaning up one end of the table and working your way to the other end.

The big picture is more of a, going around in circles idea, while generally, but not always, playing straight, or near straight in shots, which allows you to "Kill" or control the cue ball and with the next ball in your sight line.

Corner-Most balls are usually blocking something.

Rolling your cue ball. "Willy-Nilly" all around the table is billiard suicide.

- #1 Pattern shooting allows easier cue ball control
- #2 Pattern shooting doesn't require strenuous cue ball control.
- #3 Pattern shooting allows some small errors or variation without fatal errors.
- #4 Pattern shooting usually allows an easier eight ball shot.

Pattern shooting is a tool. You use it when it applies. A good example is if your opponent, at eight ball, commits suicide by shooting all or almost all of his balls, which gets them out of your way and he then turns the table over to you, by a miss or a scratch. A good pattern player is a favorite to run out.

The famous eight ball saying is, "Don't run seven if you can't run eight". If you do run seven and not eight, you just make your opponent look like a better player, as you removed all of his barriers to the pockets and obstacles in his position pies.

There are many games where you may not be able to establish a perfect pattern that will use all eight balls and out. Some times you may link up three balls and then connect to a five-ball pattern to finish up. Look for two or three ball patterns, which will help you, run out.

Often there may be more than one pattern that may work. If you have jawed balls or clusters, you may not have a pattern at all, and have to go into, "Make a ball, break a ball" mode.

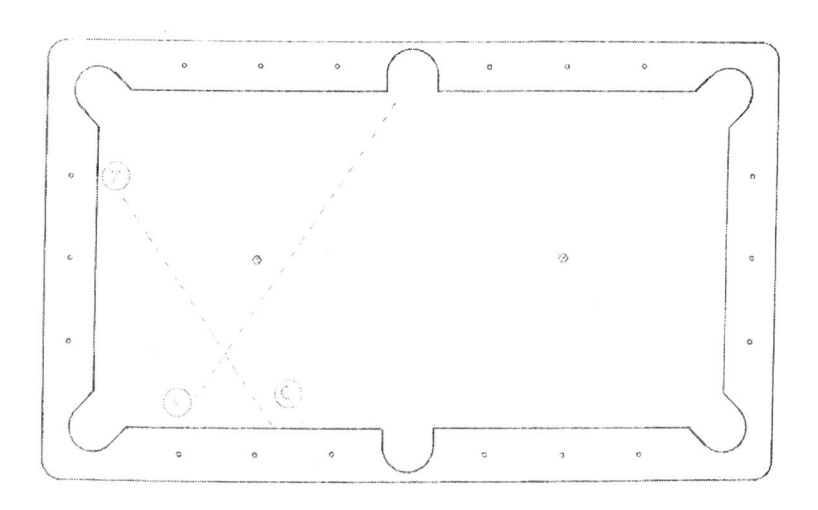

6 and 7 balls

If you had to pocket these two balls, in the above illustration, and we are assuming that they can both be made from the current cue ball's position. Would you shoot the seven and then the six, or would you shoot the six followed by the seven?

Instinctively most players correctly pick the six and then the seven, but have a hard time expressing why. Relax, don't hurt yourself, I am going to tell you why.

By shooting the six and just staying in the six's vicinity, you are already in the position pie shaped area for the seven ball.

If you shoot the seven first, you have to know something about speed and stroke to get into the six's position pie. Common sense applies all around. This is an oversimplification of pattern shooting.

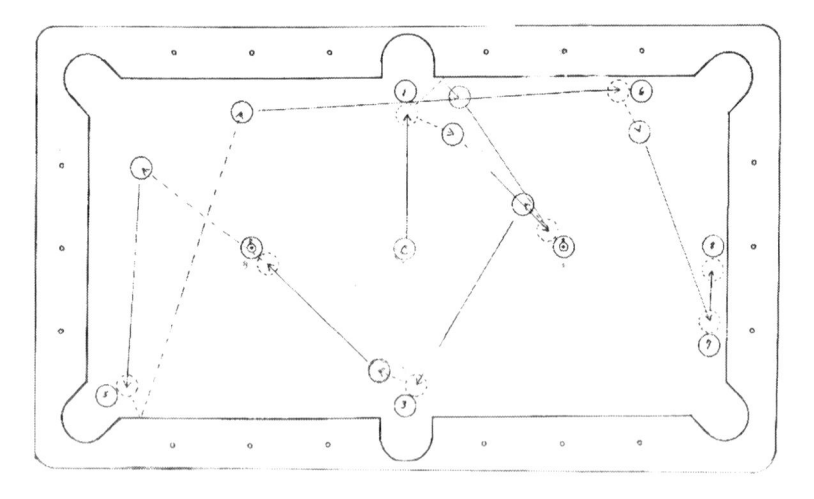

8 ball pattern again

BACK TO THE PATTERN TEST

If you had tried this run, with out knowing the "Jedi" mind trick you, in several runs, would have had trouble with the two ball and the four ball.

The two and the four are as physically far from a pocket as they can be. If you move them in any direction, they will be getting closer to some pocket or other.

Now we have some idea of what is our overall strategy. Let us try this same run from the beginning. Mel, our friendly cue ball, is in the middle of the table and is "Fired Up", and champing at the bit. If I shoot the one and stop there, I have a pretty good shot at the two-ball. If I look ahead to the three-ball and on to the four-ball, I can anticipate what kind of "Line Position" I am leading into. I can see that even though I will be in the three ball's pie, when I shoot the two ball, I would like to improve on it a little. As the thinking part of this equation, you must be prepared to improve within any position pie area, to allow for better line position for all following shots in that pattern.

So to accomplish that, I go back to the one ball shot. Now when I shoot the one ball, instead of stopping dead, I hit the one ball about a half a ball on the two ball's side roll into the side rail and bounce back toward the two ball slightly to the left of the straight in line between the two ball and the corner pocket.

Now when I shoot the two, with draw, my cue ball will drift back and to the right of where the two ball was, and also back toward the middle of the table, but not too far. I know the four ball is on the head spot and I want to be about straight in on it. I now shoot the three ball with a relaxed draw that will arrive at the three with about three or four inches of draw, and I will hit the three ball about one or two-thousandths of an inch to the right of center. The result, with practice, will be a cue ball that draws straight toward the four ball, about four or five inches away from where the three was. The four ball we just follow through, the four-ball position, with a roll shot. We want the cue ball to go down toward the head rail so we can cut the five ball thin, on the left side and improve the cue ball in the six ball's position pie. So now we shoot the five, cutting it thin and rolling the cue ball over toward the rail that the six is on. We wanted the six to be almost straight in so we can absorb all the cue ball's energy into it. This line position action allows us to shoot the six ball with a simple, relaxed draw, stop shot, which lines us up on the seven ball. After shooting the six ball, we soft roll the seven ball shot and are now in the proverbial "Cat Bird Seat", on the eight ball.

Shoot the eight ball and yell, "Winner, Winner, Chicken Dinner", all the Las Vegas players know that, "Black Jack" victory cheer.

The description is a little wordy, but I got you there without missing, and the position shots were well within your skill level, and there is no blood on the table or floor. You may have to practice the three ball shot a few times to get the feel of the soft draw to the right. Hit it at various speeds until you get it right.

Does it make any sense? Sure it does. You can sneak around the table, under complete control, and it looks like you are stealing the balls they are disappearing so fast. You can run this rack 4 or 5 times and you will be bored, rightly so. There is only so much to learn from this exact pattern. You have climbed this mountain, what is next?

PRACTICE PATTERN DRILL

Chalk up; you will like this next one. Rack all eight balls like you would for nine ball, in a diamond shape. You only have eight balls, so just leave the last, or tail ball out. Put the eight ball in the middle of the rack. Push the rack forward until the eight ball is over the foot spot.

Just do it, as it will work better. Don't worry about getting it perfectly; it doesn't matter for this exercise.

While breaking this rack, waste energy in two directions at the same time. Don't just casually break, but use your normal, A1, break stroke, stance, follow through and force.

Spot any ball that goes into a pocket, near that pocket that it just went into, but don't block other balls. It is your practice. If you want to move balls, to eliminate clusters or jawed balls, that is your call.

Pick up the cue ball. Your purpose is to recognize and then execute patterns. Start with the eight ball, mentally, and work your way back. If you don't like a break or scatter of the balls, rack again, don't waste your time trying to figure out a bad break or scatter. If you want to move balls, to eliminate clusters or jawed balls, that is your call. Your first shot is from the "cue ball in hand" position.

Start to make two or three ball pattern connections; maybe a 4 or 5 ball pattern will jump out at you. Don' get discouraged if you don't come up with a pattern that uses all eight balls, it will come in time.

Do not lose track of the overall concept. Why are you doing this? Do not get tied up in minor details. Pattern shooting will also help your straight pool game, if you ever play that.

If you make a small mistake and don't get the position that you wanted, shoot again. Move the cue around to suit you. It is your practice. Often, in practice games, I will see players make a wrong position and then try to shoot from that wrong spot. That is a waste of time and effort.

You are the part of this exercise that has the brain. Move the ball and try again.

BANKING

If I don't write something in here about banking, you are going to yell at me. Since I am very sensitive, I bow to your wishes.

I will tell you what you don't expect. Dozens of perspective students have said, "Doc, teach me how to bank."

After a lifetime of poolrooms, bars, bowling alleys, you can imagine my, smart mouthed, answer.

"I will teach you how to play right and then you won't have to bank". I mostly get a stupid or disgusted look, or sometimes a semi-valid counter, "Smart Mouthing" right back.

We always remained friends though, as after this exchange I would then go on to elaborate, on, and on, about banking, until their eyes glazed over.

Banking, based on pool table physics, is a pure art form. Other than writing a bad check to your bookie, and convincing him that it is good, banking is the most artistic action that you can perform on the pool table. I could bore you to tears with all the variables that you have to control to be a good banker. Again I will reference Robert Byrne's, Standard Book of Pool and Billiards, for some of those details.

I will interrupt myself here to name some of today's "Young Gun" Bankers and some others, not so young. John Brumback, 2010 Derby City Champ, Jason Miller, Brian Gregg, Shannon Daulton, Truman Hogue, Freddie Bentivegna, Glen "Piggy Banks" Rogers, Louie DeMarco, Efren Reyes, and Ike Runnels. Two great bankers, that have passed on are, Chicago's, Leonard "Bugs" Rucker and Cincinnati's Joey Spaeth.

There are other great bankers out there. I have only named a few from the top of my memory.

Let me share my Bohemian Artist, banking ideas.

First, only bank when it is absolutely necessary, or if you happen to be playing banks, or if it is a partly cloudy day, ha.

Second, every little variation that you apply to your cue ball, will affect your bank shot. I am talking about simple one rail, bounce backs here, long rail or short rail. Any English, Top, Draw, Right, Left, or None, in combination or not, will all cause variations in your bank results. Any speed change affects the angle of the bank.

Preacher Feeney sells a banking tape in which he shoots the same bank shot over, and over, and over, with all of the variations that apply. It takes about forty-five or fifty minutes, but covers that one shot completely so you should understand it when done.

So if you decide to teach yourself how to bank, and there is nothing wrong with that, Start with a very simple bank and shoot it with no spin at all, and about the same speed on each try. Hit this same shot over and over until confident, then gradually induce changes, of speed and/or spin, and observe the results.

The cushions look like a straight line, and they are until you hit them with the sphere shaped target ball. You may easily fall into a trap.

The cushion is just like a mirror, which is not perfect. Imagine a mirror sitting on top the cushion, just at the edge you are going to hit with the ball that you are trying to bank. Now you imagine looking into that mirror and you just mentally shoot the ball into that pocket reflected in your imaginary mirror. If you shoot softly that may work, but as you increase to speed of the stroke, the curved surface of the object ball distorts the straight line of the rail.

Now take an object ball and push it firmly into the closest cushion. Can you see the cushion distortion? See how the straight line of the rail is curving around the outside surface of the ball? Imagine the ball coming into the rail, at an angle, from one direction. Now imagine it going away from the rail in the opposite direction and angle.

Do you realize that the surface of the cushion on the ball's outgoing, ball side has changed and it is distorted slightly so that the ball will bank short of its intended line or target? The added force of the incoming ball cups the rail and causes it to bank at a shorter angle than what your common sense logic would expect.

Good bankers use that to their advantage. They build that into their estimating of the shot, before they shoot it. As you hit the same

The Barefoot Cue Ball

bank shot harder and harder, you will observe it slowly gets shorter and shorter.

The great bank players have a tendency to hit all cross-banks with about the same speed. They hit them medium-hard.

When I first noticed this I was a little confused by all this apparent slamming of the bank shots. As I observed and analyzed, the answer made sense. By using this harder than normal speed, consistently, they get a constant rail cupping that they can depend on. If you slide the object ball into the bank rail, it will bank shorter than if you roll the object ball to the same spot on the bank rail. Try this and see the difference.

They then hit some practice banks on each different table and mini-train their subconscious as to how that particular table "Banks".

Since any small adjustment in speed or English can and will vary the outcome angle of the shot, you can see where I get the artistry angle. In the heat of some competition, you can't stop to calculate and analyze before each shot. You must get on a pool table and shoot a large number of banks, while adding all of the different nuances, one at a time, so you can, get ready, "Artistically Feel" the bank shot and know it is right before pulling the trigger.

You may get that similar feeling in a poker game. You need a card to fill that straight or flush or full house, and when it comes, you are not surprised, as some part of your mind, just had the "Feeling" that the right card was there.

When you start practicing banks shots with all the various trimmings, your very powerful subconscious mind is storing all that information away. If you shoot enough, you will get comfortable with this info and before you know it, you may overhear, "That's Spanky, and he's a pretty good banker.

Remember that impossible kick shot on the eight ball to win the match, it happened and you knew it as soon as you hit it. We have all felt that syndrome working. Start practicing now and "May the Force Be With You".

Two and three rail banks are fun and they give you a bigger picture feel of the whole table. I always recommend that my training players get exposed to Three Cushion Billiards. You may never get to be a great three cushion player, but it sure will help your overall billiard education and when stuck some where due to a safety or a position mistake, it may help you avoid giving up, "Ball-In-Hand"

Fast Freddy, is better at two rails, one-pocket banks, than he is at long straight in shots. He and I are both mildly upset about that situation, but for different reasons, ha.

PINCH BANK

A pinch bank is a straight back one rail shot where you cannot get the cue ball out of the way due to the banks angle is too short.

Load up the cue ball with sidespin on the same side that you are banking the ball towards. If you are banking to your right, use right spin, if you are banking to your left, use left spin.

Now deliberately over cut the cue ball as if you wanted to bank it past the target pocket. Now hit it HARD. The HARD part cups the rail.

The English part pulls the ball back towards you. These two actions cause the ball to be "Pinched" back to a shorter angle, where it doesn't want to go, and the cue ball gets out of the way. You look like a genius.

Obviously you will have to shoot a few of these to perfect the action, speed and stroke. When I say to hit it hard, you can't slam it. Maintain your body lock stance.

The stroke must be smooth. I know it sounds odd, but don't give up. Practice a few, and remember a smooth stroke makes the English bite better. Firm and smooth works well.

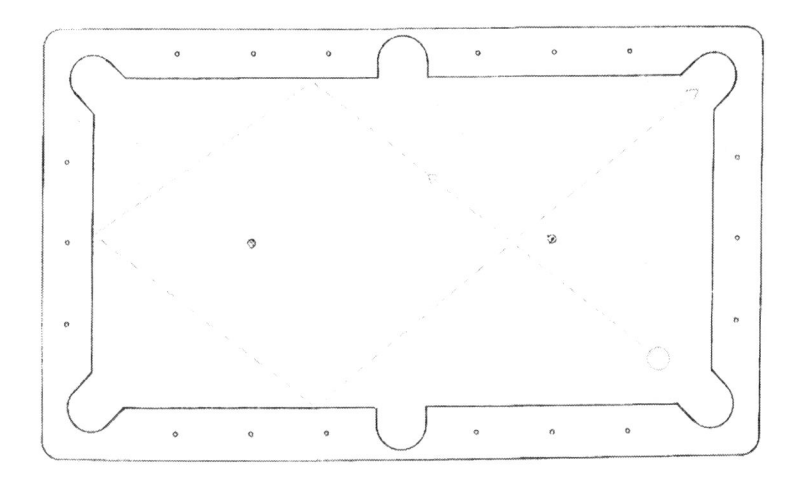

A simple 3 rail education

A SIMPLE THREE-RAIL EDUCATION

Put your cue ball in the jaws of a corner pocket, at the head of the table, as pictured above. Set the cue ball out, 5 or 6 inches away from the pocket so that you can hit it comfortably. Shoot into the lower half of the opposite rails anywhere between the 2nd and 3rd spots from the foot rail. Hit a few and get the feel of your target. You are trying to go three rails into the corner pocket on the other side of the head rail.

Start out with a sliding cue ball. Slide it all the way into the first rail. Now it is time to observe and learn, yes, again. Using a clock face as an English reference, work your way around the cue ball's English clock face. Shoot each English spot 3 or 4 times to establish consistency. Each time you change the English you will observe a different result. You are, again, teaching yourself. The variable results are scary enough to force you to practice so you will learn to control them.

I still stand by my attitude, of avoiding banks, but hey partner let's you and I practice a few of these "Bad Boys" so that when our opponent leaves us in a safety position, we can reach back into our "Jedi" mind storage and pull out that great "Feels Good" bank or kick shot, and collect what ever the prize may be!!

Paul A. "Doc" Rutter

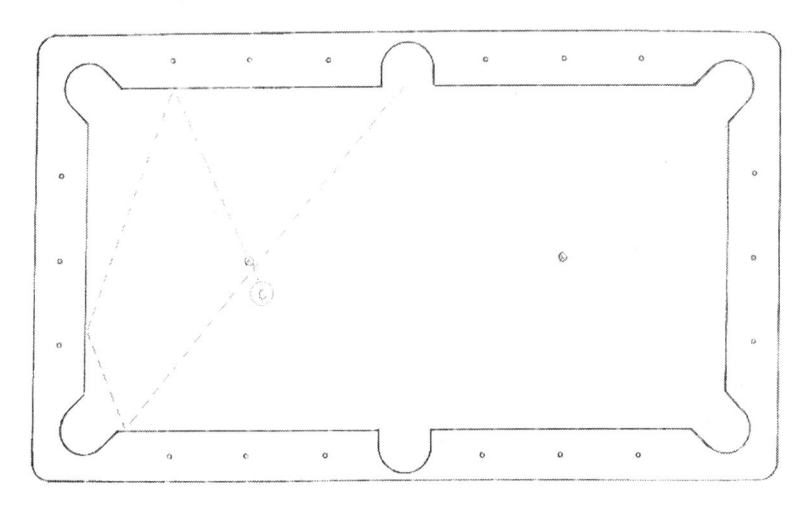

Short 3 rails in the side

Shot from the foot spot area; make any slight adjustments that are required Spot a ball on the foot spot and work on your 3-in-the-side shot. From that same foot spot shoot into the first foot rail diamond. We are using the cue ball just to give you the idea. Did you hit the long Three-in-the—side? Golf pool players love that one.

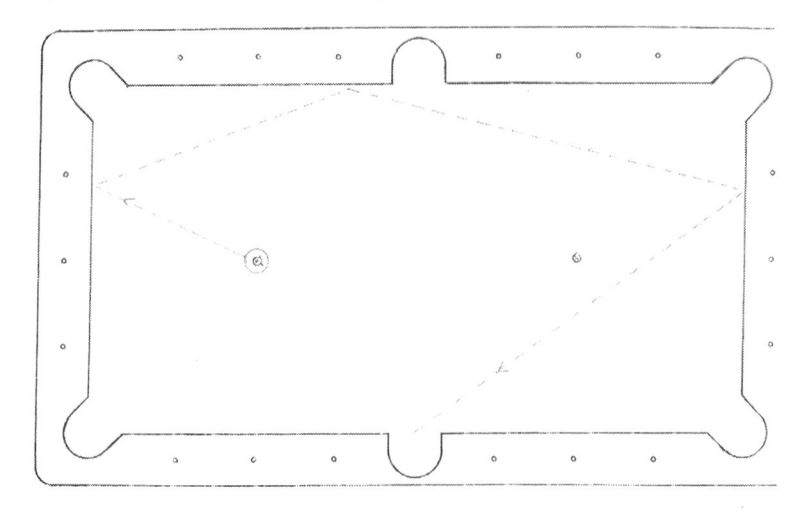

Long 3 rails in the side

If you get a chance, go to the Derby City Classic, in January, of each year. It is held at the Horseshoe Casino Southwest of Louisville Kentucky, across the river in Indiana.

I will point out the great bankers in this country for you to watch. They are playing in the tournament and also in the side room cash games until the wee hours.

Banking tip. Don't play banks with old black guys from Chicago, or young white guys from Indiana, Ohio or Kentucky, **period.**

SMALL TABLE EIGHT BALL AMERICA'S GAME

You must be a master position player, and a competent strategist to play small table eight ball well.

The Pro Players have been beating their heads against the wall for years. They have been trying to attract normal people to pay money to watch them play nine-foot table, nine ball.

Those watching people soon get bored after their first experience and don't come back, nor do they speak well of the experience. After a few racks, nine ball is sort of like watching paint dry. Non-players don't understand the hidden cue ball magic.

Okay, I'll admit it, I have played nine ball all of my life, but only with some incentive, Cash, Ego satisfaction, Thursday afternoon Car Wash Title, etc. The game itself soon grows boring and repetitive. Yeah, I can count to nine.

What am I up to? I am not trying to insult Professional nine ball players. Most of them play nine ball, as there is no choice. They play what is being promoted. I don't need several nine-ballers yelling at me, so calm down, I'm going to try and "Splain" something to yah.

The Ten-foot tables got phased out when World War two came along. The nine-footed ones are dwindling down.

The eight foot ones mostly ended up in residents, or recreation rooms. Most of us agree that the six-foot table is too small to even fold laundry on.

The final compromise is, The Infamous, 40" by 80", seven-foot table. The seven foot table is big enough to hold the balls, small enough to wrap your competitive brain around, and you only need the mechanical bridge for a very few shots.

Small, medium, and large town America is filled with the "Devil's" tool. I mean that ornery little seven-foot table. They are in every bar, bowling alley, recreation center, and church basement and they are set up to play EIGHT BALL.

Eight ball takes a different mind set to play it right, and then you will be lucky to be two thirds successful. I stated at the top of this section that a player has to be a master position player and a competent strategist to play Eight ball well. What is different? Well, Alphonse, how much time do you have. Pull up a chair, and let's talk.

If we play nine, or ten ball, Rotation, One-Pocket, Straight Pool, (14-1 or line up). Any player from either side may shoot an "ON" ball in the rotation games, and play any combinations starting with that same "On" ball. Those players may shoot any ball on the table in the other games.

In eight ball, each side has it's own balls. Not only can't you shoot the other guys balls, but also the "Doggone" things are in my way. I have to develop a strategy to deal with these obstacles. He gets a "good hit" on his ball, and then hides me behind it. You may argue the merits of the differences, and similarities till sun-up, but here is the big picture.

Grandma has heard and understands the language of eight ball. The Eight Ball Games Vernacular is in our everyday language. She understands, "he's behind the EIGHT BALL". "Stripes or Solids" (everyone knows what you mean), "Don't run seven if you can't run eight", etc. Guess what? Grandma has never hit a ball, but she knows and is interested, and would probably watch it on TV or pay to see a Tournament. Blocking pockets with your balls is a viable strategy that is not in the other games. She may even discuss a player's safety strategy, or lack thereof. I tell you. "It's America's Game"!!

I have been a poolroom rat since I was thirteen years old. We played in Al Renner's Pawnshop. Just off of Third Street in Coshocton, Ohio. Nine ball was a nickel a rack and eight ball, or rotation was a dime.

Economists that we were, two nickel nine ball racks equaled eighteen balls to the other one game's fifteen. We played nine ball.

The Barefoot Cue Ball

In the early 1970's, we moved from the Washington, D.C./Baltimore, Maryland area into the Twin cities of Minnesota. My brother-in-law, Mike Kelley, a fair bar player, says to me, "Come on, play pool in our Eight ball league"

I was shocked when I saw, seven foot tables, (postage stamp), eight ball, (a kids game), and big, fat, two and three eighths diameter cue ball. Is this for real?

Okay, how hard can it be?

Thirty-five years later I will defend the seven-foot table, and eight ball as the hardest game in pocket billiards to play well.

I attended 3 IPT tournaments. I was there every day. I made an astounding observation. The very best Professional players in the world, playing eight ball, had a statistical win record of about sixty five percent. Check it out. Bet on it.

From Efren Reyes and on down. They lost thirty five percent of their games, due to, in most part, the complexity and circumstances of eight ball.

What are the game stoppers? Some were dry breaks, no shot after the break, blocked pockets, not enough tools to clear them, safety play, clustered balls with not good enough tools to break them out, etc.

MINOR STRATEGIES AND SPURIOUS INFO

Nine ball favors an aggressive, offensive ball firing mode. Eight ball favors a more conservative approach, leaning to an almost defensive posture on occasion. Tactics that are designed to avoid mistakes are favored over, who can make the most balls quickly.

Eight ballers learn to sneak around the table playing exact position control shots, avoiding the obstacles of their opponent's balls, and or breaking up clusters and obstructing balls, as they go merrily along to their final task, shooting in the eight ball. These same tacticians are like a sniper, just waiting for you to make a mistake, BANG, you're dead. Great fun, but it can some times be tedious.

The winner of an eight ball match may simply be the player that made the fewest mistakes. A good offensive safety, at the right time is better than a low percentage bank or low confidence combination. I will talk about safeties later on.

I am a proponent of shooting the, "wrong ball at the right time". Imagine a trouble ball. It can't be made until it is banked or broken out. I may take the wrong, harder shot, early in the rack, which allows me to solve that problem ball situation. Hence, the phrase, "Shoot the Wrong Ball at the Right Time".

Lancy Howard in "The Cincinnati Kid" stated, "That's what it's all about kid, making the wrong move at the right time".

If I can lower my opponents probabilities of success by subtly moving his balls to less advantages positions, with a thin kiss shot or, a cue ball carom, I definitely will.

Imagine an opponent's ball very near a side pocket that can be easily made. I may be able to shoot past that ball, but if a thin kiss will move it down the side rail, just a few inches, and it may even cluster up with another ball, I will do it, while still pocketing my ball. That action also helps my confidence level as I proceed to run out. If I do get in trouble or make a mistake, I have lowered his probability of success and required him to play at a higher level to win.

When an opponent, first at the table, runs five to seven balls, and doesn't get out, the first thing you look at is the eight ball. Is it open? Do I have to break or bank it?

The next thing I look at is where are my opponent's balls located. If his balls are jawed, or clustered or in the end zone, I immediately gain confidence as his ball may be so bad off, that with a safety or two, or just by shooting the balls in the right pattern, I may get out with very little risk.

Running an eight ball rack is a series of tasks. The easier shots are your tools that allow you to solve your problems and win. If you have more problem balls than tool balls, don't just keep on mindlessly pocketing those easier shots and hope for some unidentified miracle to let you out. That's why pawnshops don't go broke.

Develop the strategy of blocking pockets, when your opponent has balls aimed that way. He can play position behind those balls, but it is harder to do it in a usually, smaller position pie area. If the task is more difficult he is more likely to fail.

If your opponent has one of his balls jawed in a pocket where you have two or three balls aimed, take the first opportunity to combo his ball in with one of yours. As long as his ball is blocking your balls, you may not be able to complete your game plan.

Always call your ball in this case as your ball may follow his in. If you can, use an offensive safety to improve the layout of some of your problem balls.

In some games, all of the strategies in the World just don't seem to work. You may have to "Grit" your teeth make that difficult cut, bank, carom, or combination and win in spite of it all, ha.

In order to run out, you must see a path that takes you all the way out. Do not get so caught up in pocketing easy balls that you forget that your purpose is to win the game. Seven great shots will not win it takes eight.

Nothing is worse than working your way down to that last shot, that is almost impossible to make, and then, after your valiant, but failed attempt, you hear, your opponent say," Nice try". You know he is following that, in his own mind, with, "for a dummy".

Anytime you approach an open rack, always walk completely around the table. Look at each ball. Can that ball be made, in a most likely pocket? Is a viable position pie available? Do any other balls lead nicely up to it?

Identify problem situations. As I work my way around, decisions start forming. Look, I can bump a ball there. I can shoot that ball into the wrong pocket, allowing a better line position on the next ball, for an easier run out. Work, work, work, and identify potential fixes for those awkward situations.

I have stated that Eight Ball is performing a series of tasks. If you are willing to put more mental effort into your game, you may find that the actual shots and winning may get easier.

Notice the difference again, between eight ball and the rotation games. In nine ball once you shoot the three ball, you have one option, go find that four ball and shoot it. In eight ball, some times the options are almost overwhelming. You must set the priorities that fit within your previously practiced abilities.

It is Your Life, your decisions, your game plan, and if you are willing to study, you will start enjoying more success. Success is usually good. The nice thing about it, is with the help of this and some other books, you may work on the overall game, one piece at a time. You don't have to master it all at once.

As you progress through a run out, always stop before a shot. Walk around the table and look ahead, imagining that you are shooting the next shot. Then the next shot after that. Always look at least three shots ahead.

This method fixes your plan into your subconscious mind, which will now help you accomplish that action. Let your mind raise the responsibility of the current shot, to help facilitate the next shot.

Too many players will look ahead, but from where they are standing. They are too lazy to go to the other side of the table and then when they get around to that next shot, they find they have come up short or long or with a wrong angle.

They are now somewhere they don't want to be. Who should they blame? Let the power of your subconscious mind work for you.

In the NFL, is the winning team playing or working harder than the losing team? I don't think so. I think the losing team maybe working harder. It is just a small theory.

In a losing pool match, did the other guy physically out work you? Probably not, but he may have mentally out thought you.

JEDI MIND TRICK

When I laughingly refer to a Jedi Mind Trick, I am really referencing a variation on the "Power of Positive Thinking". I know I am not a real Jedi master, but shh, don't tell my opponent that. It may give me an edge; even a small one helps a little bit.

While shooting, always visualize success. The power of your subconscious mind, which at some point knows how to play, will support your billiard artistic/physical actions, to the degree necessary, to accomplish the simple tasks, during the course of a simple billiard stroke. Picture the target ball actually going into the target pocket. Does that sound silly? It works!!

Think about it. Educated folks, far smarter than me have figured out that the "Choking" syndrome is caused by, the scared part of your brain picturing the ball hitting somewhere other that where you want it. While, in a bolder part of your mind, the hero section, says, "Leave me alone, I know what I am doing. And as the argument rages, a third part of you mind, the "What me worry" part, says, "I don't have time for this crap, my opponent is waiting, I see what you want" and pulls the trigger on the failing picture that you just displayed to whatever part of the mind that is paying attention.

Did you miss? That is what you showed your mind, that you wanted to do!!! I say again, ALWAYS VISUALIZE SUCCESS.

Bring the Power of Positive Thinking into your game.

This brings us to another, related aspect of the game. Oh no, Ernie moans, he is going to talk about focus.

FOCUS

Focus is one of those items that dictate the outcome of a match, more often than not. Incentive may create focus, but not the other way around. There is a definite relationship.

Bert and Ernie are daily players that share a "balls pocketed per inning" average of two and a half. They overhear Ace and Deuce; the rooms best two players discussing a recently finished match.

Deuce opines, "I thought I was a duster until you missed that seventh ball". Ace replies, "I had you beat so bad, that in my mind, I was already spending your money, and I lost my focus".

Days later Bert and Ernie are now talking about, "Losing their focus". They are really not sure what it means, but it sure sounds good, as an excuse for losing.

You can't let up, mentally for even a part of a second. The approach to a billiard shot is a series of sightings and info storing, and referencing of small bits of information. Find the target ball. Find the target pocket. Line them up with you.

Crouch into your "body lock" stance. Loosely short stroke your cue stick to assure all parts of your mind that nothing is impeding your shot.

While this is going on, you have also cranked into that powerful mind set, your cue ball positioning info. How high or low do I hit the cue ball? Is there any sidespin required? If so, what mini compensations have to be adjusted for?

Once the position information is settled. That info goes into your temporary mind storage. Unless for some reason, you change your mind, don't revisit it.

The fundamental of, stance, arm swing, (stroke), bridge, that you have practiced for hours, now takes over this portion of the shot. You have already trained your mind for the execution of this action. Now switch to ball hit mode.

Within a small area, on the curved surface of the object ball, there are dozens of spots, within a few thousandths of an inch from each other that you can hit, but there is probably only one of those that will satisfy your mental success, picture.

Slowly mentally eliminate the surrounding world. Hover over the shot until you have eliminated all but the one magic spot you are trying to find on the target ball's surface. The cue ball still exists, but not at the top of your mind set. Those decisions have been made. **Do not shoot until your whole mind is satisfied**.

Then, **"Stay down and follow through"**.

Train your mind, piece by piece, to do it right. Do all your thinking first. At shot time, listen to your internal music and let the stroke flow, Tah Dah!!!

PAUSE STROKE

I must add an embellishment to your normal shooting stroke. It is an option. Players each have their own number of false, or warm up strokes that are accomplished before the actual, final, shooting stroke.

Try this variation. I think it has value. On the last warm up stroke, and you are ready to go now. Pause with your cue all the way back, at the extreme end of your backstroke. Just for enough time to make sure that you have all information in "GO" mode. How long do you pause? Not long, only your own practice will tell you that.

At the focus point you are like a submarine captain, at the periscope, honing in on a target, constantly assessing and processing info, towards a mental satisfaction point. A slightly fuzzy image starts to get fine-tuned. Like a thirty-five millimeter camera, with a focusing ring that you tune in slowly, while searching for that perfect image.

Although it takes a while to write and to read this, it actually happens in a very small time period.

Focus is an easy word to define and say, but hard to project into an exact mental image as it applies to a pocket billiard shot. When your focus is working, you will know it. You will start and complete the billiard stroke with total confidence. You may occasionally wonder, "Why can't I do that every time"? You can, but it isn't easy.

Many things can and will interrupt this focusing process. Your pal, standing in front of your target pocket weaving and wiggling, is trying to destroy your focus, or that sexy lady, right in your line of sight, that keeps crossing and uncrossing those beautiful, short-skirted legs.

Paul A. "Doc" Rutter

THE ZONE

You will hear players talking about being in the "Zone". The zone, as it relates to pool, is a semi-subconscious state of mind where the player is so focused on the game and shots that he is unaware of, casual conversations, area noises, doors opening or closing. The focus point is not a time for a lot of thinking. You have been doing that right up till now. Your subconscious mind takes over and fine focuses and fires. Swoosh were you surprised?

In one bizarre case a Pizza Delivery, across the street, from a local bar/poolroom, supposedly sharked a player, causing him to miss a shot, at least that is the story we were told, right Mike?

Had that player been in the ZONE he could have eaten the Pizza and not even remembered it. Players can and will blame various distractions for taking their focus away. If you are in the zone, you are in your own little world and NOTHING distracts you.

You lucky dog, I have a small zone story for you. Several years ago I was in Hartford, Wisconsin. I was visiting a well-known cue maker "Nubs" Wagner of Nova Custom Cues. We ate at the "Mineshaft" and after, as folks like us will do, we wandered into, a three pool table bar, in which "Nubs" played weekly league pool.

I got embroiled in a five dollar; nine ball game, in which each player, taking turns would challenge each winner. Four or five players were rotating. My experience as an instructor along with my observation of their skill level convinced me that, if the game lasted long enough, I couldn't lose.

Imagine my surprise, when a short time later, I was behind over a hundred bucks. This was due to nine balls flying in on the break, and several short rack combinations, such as two into the nine or three into the nine.

Without realizing it, the power of my subconscious mind slowly took over and as time went by one guy dropped out, then another. It got down to one guy and me.

We started pressing the bet. Five became ten. Ten became twenty.

I remember making the nine and picking up the money, making the nine and picking up the money, and then some time later, he muttered, "Let's play for Fifty".

All at once, just before closing time, my opponent says, "I need a favor". I replied, "What's that"? He said, "I have to owe you that last fifty.

I was stunned. I had lost track of time, I had zoned out. I have almost no remembrance of the games played or the time spent playing. I have glimpses of making the nines and picking up the money. At the end, I had all my money back and quite a bit of theirs. The best part of the story is, about a month later; my friend "Nubs" collected that last fifty bucks, for me.

How is that for a plan coming together? Being in "The Zone" is a wonderful experience. It cannot be just called up at any time. Certain condition will raise the priority of an action so that action becomes so important that your mind partially blocks out all minor influences and lets the main action take almost total control. It would be wonderful to just turn it on whenever, but it is not that simple. You get there by being so interested in what you are doing that you really couldn't care less about any other outside activity or noise in the room. When in the zone, if the poolroom catches on fire, they may have to lead you out, ha.

Incentive can and will create focus. That is when you want to beat someone so bad, that your mind clears of clutter and you are just pocketing the balls, and marking the score. You are zoning man!! For a serious player that is utopia.

Back in the sixties, at Weenie Beanie's, Jack & Jill Cue Club, in the middle of a Nine-Ball Tournament, Bernie Swartz, from Pittsburgh, was sighting down his cue at an important shot. This nice looking lady, sitting at tableside, on the same floor level, was right in line with the shot.

Just as Bernie was about to stroke the shot, she bends down and looks right up the cue's shaft back at Bernie. He stiffened like he had been shot. His body and facial reaction was hysterical. It took a while to settle Bernie down, along with the whole room.

The referee had to tell the lady, Please don't do that. She had the proverbial "Bird's eye view" and Bernie almost had a heart attack. I will just bet that Bernie has never forgotten that small incident.

INCENTIVE

Incentive has two sides, both good and bad. Good incentive can occur when you want to beat an opponent so bad, that you lock mentally, zone out, and "Shoot The Lights Out".

Our best player, Ace, has been beating Cashmere, his long-suffering and less talented friend, for several months. Along comes the "Cracker Barrel 500" pool tournament. They draw each other.

Cashmere goes into mental cleansing mode and remembers previous matches, in which he usually lost.

Ace has already dismissed Cashmere, in his own mind, as any threat. And he starts to look ahead on the schedule, to see if there is anyone that is going to be tough.

Cashmere grits his teeth and brings out his good incentive thoughts, (I am not shooting until I am locked in. I'm tired of him beating me like a drum, and then calling me "Bongo". I will not, I absolutely will not make any mistakes).

He is working on his good incentive.

Ace is thinking too. (Ho Hum, it shouldn't take long to blow this fish away, he should probably just concede and save the time, I wonder if I can talk him into a side bet, I will have to give him odds of coarse).

You guessed it. Cashmere, "Beats Ace like a rented Mule", and Ace is trying to figure out how he could possibly have played that bad.

Cashmere pumped up, Ace let down. The local Sweaters are in a tizzy.

You have probably seen variations of this syndrome. Did it happen to you? How bad do you want to win? Nobody loses on purpose, but at times you may not want it enough to sustain the focus that you need for normal execution.

Even in practice, if you are just slapping balls around, stop. You can't afford to teach your subconscious mind those bad images. That kind of stuff can and will jump up and bite you like an attack trained toy dog.

Good or bad, I always found money to be a strong incentive factor. Until I moved to Minnesota, there was always some cash action in the game. In Minnesota I got involved in league play with no side action. It is tough to keep your mind in focus when you are playing for free. Did I say free? They make me pay league dues and Green Fees, every week.

Years ago, I was asked, "Why are those Philippine guys so damn good? The answer I gave is obvious. Beginning players, in their formative years, played for money right from the start. If they lost it may mean eating out of and sleeping next to a dumpster. That's INCENTIVE.

American amateurs, in their formative years mostly played for free, win or lose; they eat well and sleep soft. Their game or match outcome usually had no monetary incentive, or negative repercussions. This, of course is a broad generalization, to support the theory.

Bottom Line, how bad do you want it?

What are you willing to invest, physical or mental to get it?

BREAK SHOTS

Years ago when the interest in Straight pool was high, a hard break was no big deal. After "The Color Of Money" in 1987, we had cue balls flying around the poolrooms like "House Trailers" in a tornado. The short rack games of eight and nine ball created a whole new atmosphere of loud cracks and even some broken pool cue shafts.

The break shot had been pretty much fortune oriented through several decades until Mike Sigal decided it needed some extra effort, expended it its direction to enhance his, already strong nine ball game.

Mike went down to visit with "Red" Jones in Pasadena, Florida, a suburb of Tampa, Florida. Red had a nice nine-foot Brunswick Gold Crown table. While Red racked the balls, Mike perfected what ever he was trying to learn about breaking. He searched the head string from one end to the other, looking for the magic spot to break from.

This intense session went on for two days, rack, and break, rack and break, over and over. Red said, "Mike got pretty good at breaking, but I am now the uncontested nine ball rack champion in the Southern half of Florida.

Mike took that newfound style into his tournament games. He would search the head string until he found the sweet spot, and then he would pound his opponents into the cloth, leaving only some blood, sweat, and chalk dust.

Along came the Sardo, Tight Rack.

Corey Deuel took one look at one of those new racks and realized that some consistency was possible in racking the balls for the first time ever. Corey used a variation on a kiss shot and figure out that by using a softer break, from the side, and a rolling cue ball, he could get that head ball to kiss back into the opposite side pocket, from the side he broke from. He could do it very consistently.

I watched Corey at the IPT tournament in Reno. He was playing a very good Chinese player. I could neither, spell nor pronounce his name so we will leave it at that.

The Chinese player was trying every thing he could, while racking the balls to stop this break magician, from breaking in a ball, every time and then running out.

The Chinese player, when racking even tried to pound on the two balls behind the head ball. Corey stopped him at that point and got a referee to tell the poor guy he had to just rack the balls normally and watch.

Corey's next match was on the TV table. He jumped on that table before his next match and with Nick Varner racking, due to the heat from the extra lighting, he couldn't get the same break to work, on the warmer, drier table

Earl Strickland quit a major tournament at Terry Romine's poolroom, in Milwaukee, over this new soft break business. Earl was playing Corey in the finals. The officials, when asked by Earl, could not stop Corey from pocketing the one ball in the side pocket, every time, with his soft break.

The emotions ran so high that Earl picked up his tack and walked out in the middle of that final match, conceding the win to Corey, who graciously accepted.

I tried Corey's break on the seven-foot tables and got it to work. I quit using it, as I could not control where the two ball was being racked and since the slow speed left the cue ball near the foot rail, it only provided limited success.

Without the Sardo Tight Rack, Corey's famous break becomes inconsistent, but it still works some times.

In eight ball, two breaks are generally used. The first is simple. Hit the head ball straight on from where ever you are shooting from, on the head string. Use a center ball slide hit, trying to arrive with no spin on the cue ball. You are trying to bounce the cue ball back into the approximate middle of the table, there by increasing the chances of you getting a shot after the break. This break gives the best overall scatter, and that makes it easier for you to run out. If you don't make a ball, it is easier for your opponent to run out. Hence the proverbial Double edged sword.

Second, if the rules reward a player for making the eight on the break, hit the second ball back, full on, from the side with some draw. You have to play with this to establish how much draw your stroke creates. The eight will sometimes go into the opposite side that you break from, or on occasion it kisses into that same side head, corner pocket. You also have to play with exactly where you are hitting the second ball back. It seems that a couple of thousandths of an inch, one-way or the other makes a difference. If I don't seem to be doing well, I will switch to the third ball back, just to shake up my opponent, who is racking the balls. The second ball break seems to scatter the balls differently than the head on break. It seems to leave more clumps and clusters, but you will usually make a ball.

A couple of variations of your handgrip on the cue may bear fruit. A shorter grip, more toward the middle of the cue stick, at the front of the wrap area will enhance the loose hand, wrist snap, along with a more upright stance, allows more speed.

A rear grip, clear back at the end of the cue, behind the wrap area, will allow a more powerful thrusting follow through. Give these both a try, to see if one or the other works for you.

If you're cue ball is flying off the table on the break shots, you are inadvertently elevating your cue stick, on the break. As you hit down on the ball, whether you wanted to or not, plus the added power, for a harder break, your cue ball is forced down into the cloth, then basic physics forces it back up from the cloth and it skips merrily down the table, and hits the head ball while in the air.

Since it is in the air, it hits the first object ball on its slanted upper slope, above the center, of the surface of that ball. The cue ball has no choice; it flies up in the air depending on the actual force of your break shot to determine its trajectory and landing, somewhere other than on the table. It is much better to level out your cue stick and possibly not hit the cue ball quite so hard, than to risk giving your opponent "Ball-In-Hand".

RACK YOUR OWN

The one-pocket players started racking their own balls, over ten years ago. That concept has trickled down to the eight ball and nine ball players. In some leagues it has become an option. Your opponent may ask, do you want to rack or me? You have to decide what you think is best. I doubt that you would give yourself a bad rack, so that is the safest. For years it was fashionable to accuse the opponent of "Bad Racking Technique". You may find out that you try to rack as best you can, and you still come up with a "Dry Break". Some players will try to use the racking as a sharking technique. By making you rack then re-rack a few times, they may try to get into your head. If a player requests a re-rack, I will accommodate him, ONCE, if he is not happy, I just hand him the triangle and walk away.

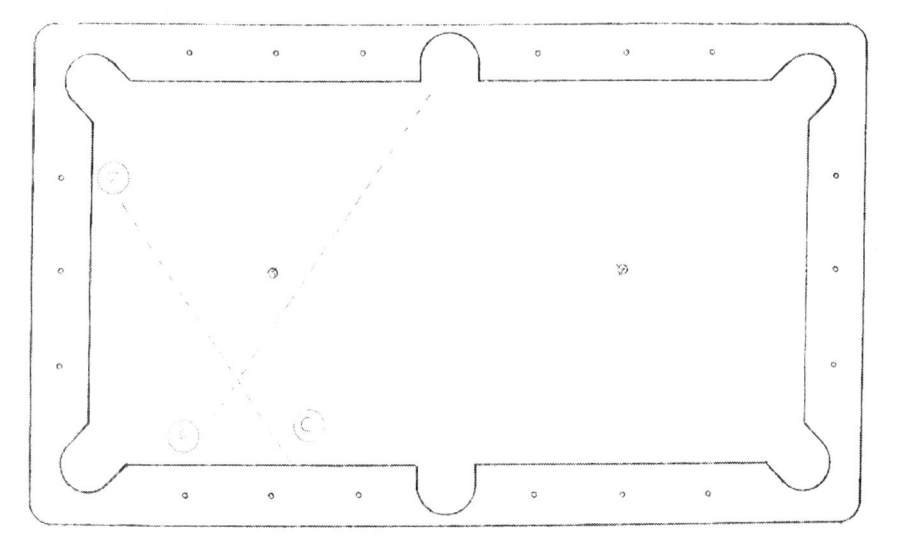

6 and 7 balls again

Look at the illustration. Common sense shows you that the six ball is a more powerful/valuable ball than the seven ball. The six ball can be pocketed from a cue ball anywhere in the large, Pie Shaped Position area. (Hence, position pie). The seven ball is in the end zone, and can only be pocketed by a cue ball in that smaller position pie.

Thousands of eight ball games have been lost by players that didn't recognize the low offensive value of balls in the end zone, and the priority of shooting those balls as soon as you can, unless they fit into a later part of a predetermined pattern. Respect end zone balls. If they are ignored, they will come back and bite you.

STRAIGHT POOL

Straight pool is to pocket billiards as practice scales are to a concert pianist. Yes, it may become boring, but it will make you a better player. The discipline of straight pool is absolute. If you fail to play position on a particular ball, every time, you pay the price of running out of good shots.

Here are some "Big Picture" tips. When using a break shot to open up the rack, try to hit one of the four corner balls in that rack. The middle balls will absorb most of the cue ball's Kinetic energy; the corner balls seem to allow a better scatter.

As you observe a table of scattered balls, try to shoot the "Corner Most" balls. By doing this you are opening paths for the "Center Most" balls that need open paths to the pockets.

Always, always, always play position on a particular ball. You don't have to shoot that ball. If a better shot comes up, go for it, but make sure you have the original "Ace In The Hole" to lead you out of the woods.

Shoot as many "Stop Shots" as good pattern play will allow.

Don't break clusters that can be cleared by selective position play.

If you just let your cue ball go, thinking, "I can shoot any ball so why worry", you will soon find your self with out a shot and wondering how you got there.

THE QUADRANT THEORY

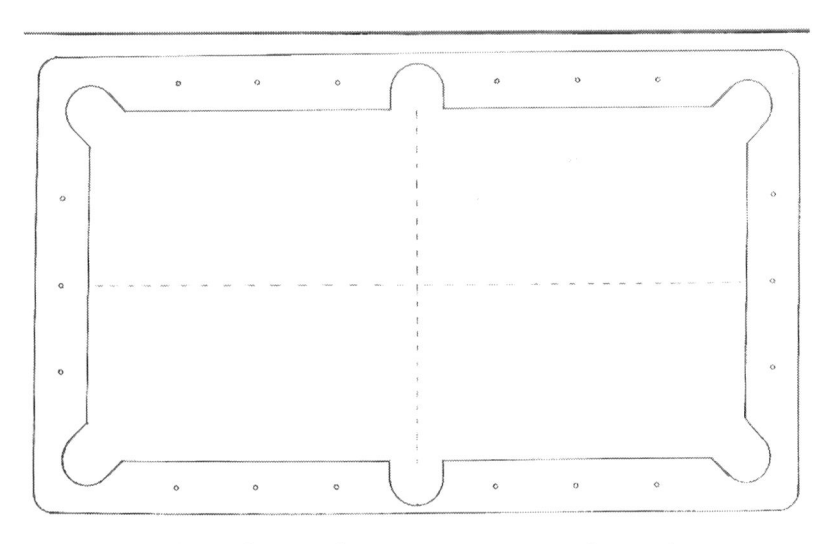

Table with center lines connecting center diamonds

Using the corner pockets as primary targets. Balls in each rectangle or quadrant will, most likely be pocketed in the corner pocket that is in that rectangle.

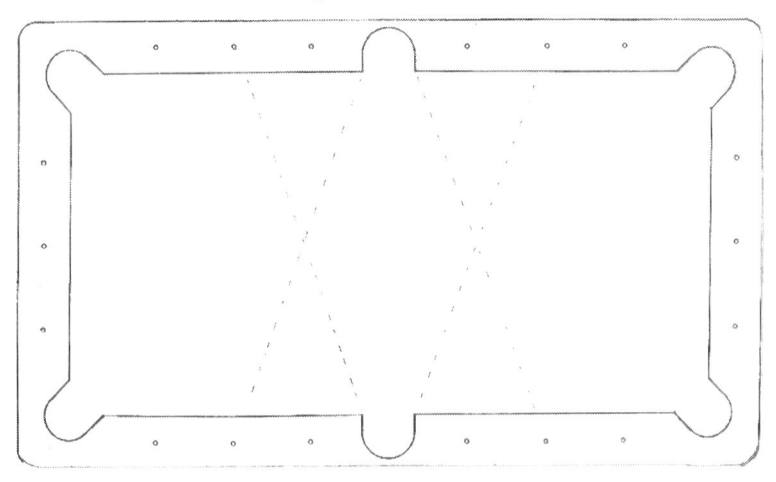

Add the side pocket football shaped area

The Barefoot Cue Ball

The football, or double wedged shaped areas are the most optimum for side pocket shots. From this area the side pockets are two and a quarter balls wide

This is heavy probability stuff; I hope I can explain it to you so you can get the big picture. Generally it is an overall evaluation or the balls on the table and what is their relative value as to whether they can be pocketed easily or not.

Probability loosely means, estimated worth, although maybe not proven. (I told you, heavy stuff). That is what you do.

When you circle the table. You are estimating your chances of successfully running out this rack of balls.

If you flunked high school algebra, don't sweat it. This is more common sense than putting on shoes to go to the mailbox in the rain.

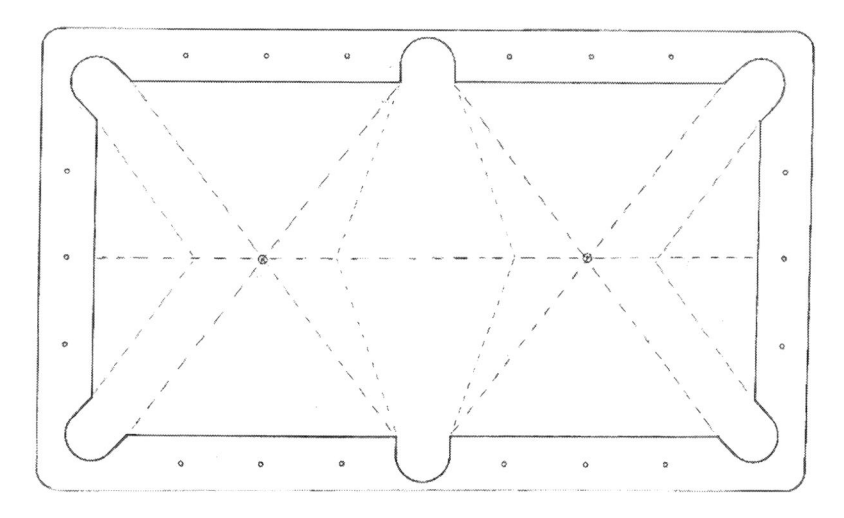

Full Tah-dah with end zones

Here is the whole Tah, Dah. This shows a wider, side pocket, double wedge area.

Note the end zones where the low value balls hide from you.

Using the corner pockets, as prime targets, in each Quadrant rectangle allows the player to make a common sense judgment of his chances of success.

Yes, I know the side pockets are there, but they are deceptive and will let you down when you depend on them. Put an object ball at various spot around the rails. Don't try to hide them behind corner rails and such. Notice that those balls can always be shot into two corner pockets.

Now line up an object ball and a cue ball, straight in to each other and straight into a side pocket. As you with your hands, sweep both balls, in a curved arc, to one side, as you approach the long side rail, eventually the object ball can no longer be made into the side pocket. The side pocket, essentially, goes away.

Many times players get paralyzed into a, "I have to shoot into the closest pocket", trap. They will be trying to shoot into an area that is way too small, which reduces their error angle to a point where they "Run out of Talent".

It may be possible for that same player to shoot that ball into a corner pocket, that is further away, but even though there is an increased error angle, the ball is actually easier to pocket. A player by adjusting his pattern could approach that same ball from a different position area, also allowing a corner pocket shot.

Mosconi, given an equal shot at either the side or corner pocket, would usually take the corner, unless it would take his cue ball where he didn't want to go, or throw him out of his current pattern.

As you, brainstorm, your way around a, spread rack table, relative ball values will become apparent. Any ball on or close to a side rail, and close to a corner pocket has a very high probability of you being able to pocket it. These balls have a relatively larger position pie, which is easy to get into with your cue ball.

Do you remember the high school math term, "Gozinto"? If a ball is shot toward a pocket with enough applied "Gozinto", you may watch as it "Goes-into" that pocket.

Yeah, I know, Shame on me. Lighten up; you were starting to show signs of serious stress, ha.

I always encourage players to circle the table and look each prospective ball into its corresponding pocket and to observe the associated position pie for each ball. This enforces the ability of your subconscious mind the help you solve your run out pattern, problems.

I could spend a lot of time reinforcing this, but you should be able to expand on this concept during your own practice, learning sessions.

Some aficionados try to work geometry into their pool games. I disagree vigorously. If your cue ball is in New Mexico and your object ball is in Virginia, that is definitely" a Geography" problem, not Geometry.

SAFETY PLAY

This is almost political. Conservative, Physics style players seem to appreciate good safeties, and Liberal, Artistic style players and drunks call it dirty pool.

Safeties played in small towns or unsophisticated bars may get you into a fight or at least a vigorous argument. Those players will, flat out say, "We don't play that kind of dirty pool around here".

League players are better educated, and they know that unscrupulous players can cheat you with the, so-called Bar rules. A "Ball in hand" penalty is harsh, but it avoids allowing an opponent to deliberately cheat you.

All of the National Pool Leagues, The V.N.E.A, the B.C.A. and the A.P.A. and the Professional Tournaments enforce the safety rules. Do you want to run with the Big Dogs? Then learn and play by the rules, or stay on the Porch.

The players in organized events know that good safety play requires skill to execute and is respected and appreciated by the highly skilled players.

Beginning, or lower level players have a tendency to think of a safety shot as a "Last Resort" option only. A safety shot becomes their, "I Give Up Mode".

A good offensive safety should be played when it will do the most good, not after all else has failed. Some players are embarrassed to play a safety if they still have a shot that can be made. If you fall into that trap, and continue to shoot any ball that you can make, even when it is obvious that you don't have the tools to get out, you are making your opponent a much better player.

The Barefoot Cue Ball

When you get your ball obstacles out of his way, you are just making it easier for him to win. You are also reducing your tools required to, run out, or play a good safety game.

In a safety game situation, the player with the most balls has the best probability of winning. That player has more places to hide, and more balls that he can hit to move his cue ball around at will.

You have been in this negative situation before. Imagine jumping on the table and running six or seven balls, but not getting out. Now your opponent has the whole table to carefully peek and hide around on with out giving you an open shot for several turns at the table. Frustrating isn't it?

Several years ago two great bar box league, and part time "Road Action" players from La Crosse, Wisconsin played in that States annual eight ball Championship tournament. The Valley National Eight-ball Association had a three foul rule in place at the time. If a player committed three consecutive fouls in a row, it was loss of game, for that player.

The two players were "Billy Steele" and Russ Lee, AKA "La Crosse Whitey". These two "Safety Bandits", and their teammates robbed so many players with the three foul rules, that they won the team event.

After the tournament was over, the VNEA threw those rules out. It caused controversy at the time, but our boys from La Crosse proved that it was a winning strategy.

At The Derby City Classic one year, "Princeton Plump", a semi-secret Kentucky player, and myself were sweating a bank match between Jimmy Reed and Bert Kinister.

It was a slow match and Bert; one bank at a time wore Jimmy out. Jimmy complimented Bert on his play. They shook hands in good spirits and parted. P.P. opined, "Jimmy didn't play very well, did he"? I replied, "You missed the game Plump. Bert was oiling (Playing Safeties) Jimmy so well, that Jimmy had almost no shots that he could make".

Later that day I caught "Princeton Plump" practicing his bank safeties.

Play safe when you should, not when you have to. For many years an easy safety was just hiding your cue ball anywhere behind a blocking ball.

Wait up a second, have you seen these short, jump cues?

Players today will leap the cue ball gaily over an obstructing ball, and laugh at your, "so called" safety.

One of my State Champion teammates, The Rosedale Flash, will make about 80 or 85 percent of his jump shots. He actually, Gasp, practices these circus freak shots. He also states, "They are Easy".

While keeping that story in mind, try to play your safeties up close to that blocking ball, so my buddy "Flash" can't jump into your bankroll!!

Do not paralyze your run-out game by excessive use of safeties. Like anything, you can go overboard. You may get so good at safety play that you are afraid to run out. Just like life, do everything in moderation.

Play safeties as long as you have balls, jawed, blocked or just difficult. As soon as you can see the open table, with your balls unimpeded, shift gears, set your pattern and start stroking for the win.

PERSONAL INSTRUCTION

Not everyone can learn from books. Most people absorb information better if the subject is something that can be demonstrated, and observed visually.

The old axiom, "One picture is worth a thousand words", certainly applies here. As an instructor, I can explain a situation and then prove it, right in front of you, with no tricks or games. A written description requires imagination.

An often repeated attitude is, "What do I need lessons for? I can just play Ace for a dollar a game and learn by watching him".

The problem with that theory is, Ace's cue ball is totally white with no features that will show how he is spinning it or why.

If Ace is asked a question, he may not have the mental acuity, or any inclination, required to explain it to you. Meanwhile Ace's retirement fund is growing.

Good players are good players; and like artists, most of them can do, but cannot explain technique to your satisfaction. It doesn't means that they are dumb, but their mind is not geared to explaining what, to them, is a somewhat natural talent.

Years ago in the 1960's, I asked Eddie Kelly, who was shooting with a 13MM shaft, why did he use that size shaft? Eddie paused and then blurted out, "Because it's better, that's why". Eddie was a first class player, and he wasn't stupid, but he probably had never given it any thought as to, " How do I explain this to a casual fan".

Later I learned the answer, but at the time neither Eddie nor I could come up with the info.

Another example of, "Great player, but not a teacher", was Ted Williams. Ted was one of the best pure baseball hitters in the game.

After he retired, he was hired as a batting coach. That surely makes sense, doesn't it?

Ted could not teach his natural talent. Could anyone?

Ted's eyes were so good that in the few seconds that it took for a baseball to leave the pitcher's hand, and arrive in the strike zone, he could see the rotation on the ball, coming at him at ninety plus miles per hour. He knew by that spin, which way the ball was going to curve, if at all. You cannot teach that!!

Earl Strickland can jump full balls with a normal, full length and full weight cue. This takes incredible hand speed to do that. I don't think that it can be taught. The concept may be taught, but not the physical stroke.

A GOOD instructor can take about fifteen years off of your normal, self-teaching, learning curve. A good teacher has the ability to explain things so that you can understand and learn to use what is being explained. Sooner than you think, a teacher will have you performing techniques that you had only dreamed about.

Don't be hustled by some local poolroom player. If he cannot explain a shot, then he is no teacher, so don't waste your money.

A good instructor sees things that a good player doesn't, and he then can explain it to you, so you can understand it!!

THREE CUSHION

When a player told me he was going to take up three-cushion billiards, I told him good. Then explained, "It is going to take you five years to learn the shots, then five years to learn how to play position, and still another five years to learn to play the safeties". Come around in fifteen years and tell me how you made out.

I do encourage players to get some exposure to three-cushion billiards. You may never be a great three-cushion player, but it surely will help you play the pocket games better and with some more confidence. It is always sexy when you get out of a hook, by shooting a three rail kick shot.

STRATEGIES

There are times when you realize that a rack is too complicated for you to run out from your current position. If by reading this book, you have learned to evaluate the overall situation, that very evaluation may cause you to decide to let your opponent shoot first. This decision was made as you may have determined that you don't think his probabilities favor him, and you would rather he make the first mistake.

This is not a bad strategy. Sometimes it works, and sometimes it doesn't. You have to have faith in your assessment. Should you be proven wrong, you must pay the price of your decision.

Should you make that decision, you can enhance your later chances by breaking up a bad cluster of your balls, on your surrendering shot. First shoot one of, the stripes or solids, which ever you choose to give you the side choice, before your surrender shot.

Another ploy that fits into this strategy is to use a Combination or carom shot to move some of your opponent's balls to a more disadvantaged position on the table.

When you approach the first shot of a new rack. Try to evaluate your chances of running out. If your balls are open, try to set a pattern in your mind and explore the feasibility of being able to accomplish the run that you have visualized. If you can't see a total full rack pattern, look for mini patterns, of three or four balls each, and a way to connect them.

If a, balls jawed, situation exists, attack that problem as soon as you can. Use your first one or two balls to set up position for a break shot. If you try for the break shot early in the run and are not successful, you now have more opportunities for another chance later. When playing a breakout shot, you will not have total control of the final path or stopping spot of your cue ball. So when breaking balls early on, there are more of your balls on the table to get lucky shape on, if your initial plan happens to have some flaws.

Players that wait until the last shot to play a critical breakout, have, game suicidal tendencies. Let's just imagine that you have waited until your seventh ball, to break out the eight ball. Here is a list of probabilities,

Make the ball, get the break, get position, and make the eight ball, and win.

Make the ball, get the break, miss position, and lose the game.

Make the ball, miss the break, and lose the game.

Make the ball, get the break, scratch, and lose the game.

Miss the ball, and lose the game.

So you can see in these real examples of what may happen, it looks like if you wait until your last chance, you only have a twenty percent chance of success.

GET those BREAKOUTS, out of the way as soon as it is possible!!

SOCIAL ORDER, GIRLS AND LEAGUES

There is usually a social Hierarchy in any poolroom, game room, etc. This is some times referred to as a "Pecking Order, as in a chicken yard.

The "A" group knows and accepts other members of that group. Their criteria: good player, acceptable gambler, good storyteller, room owner or manager.

The "B" and "C" groups loosely defined as somewhat less in all areas.

Final group the absolute beginners and strangers. I had a sign in one of my poolrooms that said, "We Cheat Tourists & Drunks". It seemed to help with this final group, ha. Some crossover continuously occurs due to gradual player skills upgrades.

There are two exceptions to this "Pecking Order". A beautiful girl may, interrupt and or join all games or conversations, at will, with no apparent penalties. Imagine that!!

If a lady is a serious player with billiard skills, her stock goes way up, as we are always looking for a Mixed Scotch Doubles Partner.

The other exception is handicap league play. Due to handicap leagues, A, B, C, & D players mix in weekly play and to some degree start to socialize over a period of time.

Lesser players are more likely to get tips from the better players who without the league exposure, would not have even talked to them before they joined the league.

This is socially healthy and enhances and expands your poolroom or game room experience. The surviving rooms today,

Paul A. "Doc" Rutter

after "The Color Of Money" died down, are benefiting from this social syndrome.

Those poolrooms that have added a full liquor bar have also gained, as in, "Hey honey how about a game for a drink"? Ha.

DRESS CODES

Playing pool is a game. A dress code, for the professional and or league tournaments is appropriate. I don't care what you look like in the bar.

Pool has just enough physical action to justify some minimal special clothing. Bowling or Golf is about the same level of physical action; so similar clothing is probably appropriate. Let's keep it simple, neat and affordable.

A nice simple, short-sleeved dress or golf type shirt for the men, along with plain semi-dress slacks, and complete the out fit, with dark colored athletic shoes.

Vests are always semi-dressy and allow for sponsor promotions. Even a hat is not out of line, if it fits into a well-known players "persona". Please, no backwards or sideways hats that just make a player look stupid rather than, cool like he envisions.

I am sure the women know what they would wear, if given a choice. My guess is the women may dress very similarly, nice blouse of their choice, similar ladies slacks and dark athletic type shoes.

Women should never be required to wear high heels, or skirts, or dresses, unless they choose to.

Over the years promoters have, on occasion, forced men players to wear suits, and tuxes, and the women to wear fancy ball gowns.

I am personally insulted by this attitude that pool players are such a poor lot that the promoter has to dress them up the make them socially acceptable for display and exhibition purposes.

Another opinion expressed by our own Rudolph Wanderone, "Putting a tux on a pool player is like putting ear rings on a pig". Alas poor Fatty, we knew him well.

Don't tell me that our game is so poorly received that our players must dress up to attract fan interest.

POOLROOM ETIQUETTE

ZANESVILLE, OHIO, THE ARCADE POOLROOM

It was in the middle fifties, downstairs, under the Arcade. The floors were wood the balls were some kind of clay composite and personal two piece cues were as rare as Chinese Jade. A good pool shot, in the nine ball ring games, was celebrated with an appreciative, "Poolroom", round of applause you guessed it. We thumped our cues on the wood floor three or four times. A direct or aside, smart mouthed comment, during the pool action, would also be rewarded with the same cue thumping accolade. About sixty years of exposure to the poolroom, sub-culture atmosphere has given me an appreciation of the, subtle, biting, ironic humor. I can usually hold my own in "Smart Mouth" with the top players authors and promoters, but will offer a fair spot of the, "seven and the breaks", to all else, ha. With this set-up, I will tell a few small stories later, that are not great stories in themselves, but they show that infamous poolroom humor we all love to share in the mid-night hours.

BILLIARD LIFE INFLUENCES

With highest respect to all

MARTHA M. RUTTER, MY MARTIE

This lady has supported my efforts in the billiard industry, with out pause, right from the proverbial "Get Go". No matter the hours I spent, or the location, or the tasks required, she was always there when I needed her. She is also not bad to look at.

When I said, "I think I will try to write a book", She said, "Well it is about time".

Martie has picked up a lot of questionable conversation habits from me, over the years, not to mention some of the things she taught my grandchildren to say, such as Uff Dah, Feda Mae, Bumbershoot, and Jitney. Yes, I had to explain to her what a "Please Don't Rain" was. I will steal a phrase from the great Jackie Gleason and declare, very sincerely, "Honey, you are the greatest".

DUARD SCHMELKE

Duard Schmelke owned and operated Schmelke Cue Mfg. in Wisconsin. They made a line of inexpensive two-piece cues that worked well for the price and they have consistently improved their cues, from the 1960's through the present time.

When he told stories, I shut up and listened. This man was a positive spirit in the early years of my cue business. He taught me the things you only learn, "From the horses mouth".

ARVED "RED" JONES

"Red" Jones played pool with five presidents of the United States. They were Roosevelt, Truman, Eisenhower, Kennedy, and Johnson.

Red, an Air Force, Full Bird Colonel, worked at the White House as an intelligence liaison for the Air Force and the CIA.

When he returned from Europe, after the Second World War, he was staying with his sister, and while she was working evenings, (she sang at the Famous Copa Cabana) Red went to one of the New York Pool rooms and ran into, played pool with, and cleaned out, (60 or 70 bucks) a guy named Jack. The next day he was introduced to his sisters friend, (Jack) who stated, "This is the SOB that cleaned me out last night shooting pool and that is why I am here trying to borrow some money from you.

Red and Jack became lifelong friends and later, when Jack became famous as "Jackie Gleason" he moved his show and his home into the Miami, Florida area.

Red lived in Pasadena, a suburb of Tampa, Florida and would go down to Jackie's about every five or six weeks and they would play pool half the night.

Red, Conrad Burkman and I are remembered at Kady's in the Riviera, by the waitresses for our "Long Winded", continuous stories, breakfasts.

Every story we told was the absolute truth, except for a lie or two!!

THE RUTTERS

Long before I came on the scene, my paternal grandfather, in the 20' & 30's had a poolroom in Wheeling, W. VA. His sons played there, in their dad's room, while they were growing up. I was informed, by one of my older cousins, H.C. Rutter of Athens, Ohio, that my dad Paul, and his brothers Harold and Ralph were competent players. They could, and did, run Sixty to eighty balls during daily straight pool play. I was born in 1939 and didn't get to see any of them play.

In my youth everyone was busy with war jobs. I listened diligently to any and all stories. By the time I was old enough to ask the questions I had, all those that had the answers, had passed on.

Thad Rutter, was an older cousin and he was known as "the Kid". He was reputed to be the best player in that part of the Ohio River Valley, for about Fifty years. Thad was one of those invited to tour with Ralph Greenleaf. Thad's dad knew Ralph's lifestyle and would not let him go.

I got to meet Thad when he was in his late seventy's, we didn't have enough time to get into his billiard history. He talked about playing Ralph Greenleaf and "Cowboy" Weston. Thad still knew his way around the pool table.

BILL "WEENIE BEANIE" STATON

In the late 1960's Bill ran two great National pool Tournaments each year. They played nine ball in one and 14-1 Straight pool in the other. I attended these in a Hypnotic Trance. My, then new wife, Martie and I were exposed to all of the current players of the pocket billiard world. The tournament fields were a "Who, Who, of all the greats, near greats, and soon to become greats.

There was more action there than in a nest of rattlesnakes on a hot rock. It was hard to decide whom you wanted to watch as you may be missing out on something else on the next table.

I will try to name a few of the players, but it was a long time ago. Luther Lassiter, Joe Balsis, Irving Crane, Richard Rigge, Eddie Kelly, "Cue Ball" Kelly, Jimmy Rempe (about 22 years old at the time) Rochester Slim, Eddie "The Hat" Burton, Baltimore Buddy (dressed like an undertaker), Bernie Swartz from Pittsburgh, Bill Incardona (who had to use a pencil to figure his bets, as we had no calculators then, ha) Howard Barrett, Richie Florence, Steve Cook, Pete Murnack, and Joey Spaeth, the Cincinnati Kid, at the time, (with proper respect to Don Willis the "Original").

Bill had purchased the "Jack & Jill" cue club from Red Jones. I was busy eying all the players; Bill seemed to be eying Martie, my nineteen-year-old bride. I teased him about it later, but being smart, he played dumb. Beanie was an action player who was pleasant to socialize with, and he would "Bet A Bunch", right now.

We became once a year friends. Bill was a "Scratch" storyteller. He would regale me with many an "Action" story as we shared a bleacher seat, at some tournament or other.

Did I tell you about the time Beanie won almost a quarter of a million dollars in Detroit, playing "Jew Paul", and his backers?

Some months later he lost back all the cash and three Cadillacs, to some other guys, in the same Detroit area.

Okay, it was the same Cadillac that he had to hock and buy back three times, to get enough cash to get "Out of Town".

The third time, Bill made his daughter go up to get the Cadillac back so he would not get talked into another trap game!!!

LUTHER "WIMPY" LASSITER

Since I already had my ticket, I didn't feel bad about sneaking into the tournament area of Bill Staton's Jack & Jill Cue club.

Luther Lassiter was practicing by himself. I eased around the wall and got up into a bleacher seat without disturbing him.

I learned three things. First thing, as a practice stroke Wimpy was hitting all shots while holding his cue, with his hand just in front of the wrap.

Over the years and after much reflection and analysis, of this technique, I determined that it was a, practice mind trick, more than anything physical. It would enhance the wrist action somewhat, but a change like he was doing will act like a clearing of the mind before the coming battle.

It tells the mind, "Pay attention, I am doing something different". Can you deal with this change and still function at a high level of competence?. I believe the technique has value. You have to decide for yourself.

Second thing. On any long shot, with six to eight feet between the cue ball and the object ball, Wimpy would "Over widen" his stance. This made immediate sense to me.

A player, particularly on a long shot, is like a tree swaying in the breeze. By over widening his stance he was not allowing his body to sway or move sideways at all. To try this, place your feet much wider apart, sideways. This will widen your stance to the point that you cannot stand back up without lurching slightly to one side.

This over wide stance makes you absolutely stable, which inspires confidence while shooting a shot that has been intimidating you. Another tip, during this particular shot, is to lower your head closer to the cue stick, like a snooker player. This seems to help with focus.

While down in this exaggerated stance you will feel your body is locked, from any swaying, and you can hold the aim point on the distant ball much better.

Now don't stroke hard, just let the weight of the cue stick flow. Try this. I will bet that long shots will not hold the fearful grip that they once had on you.

Third thing. Oh right, I can't imagine why any one ever tried to play "Wimpy" for money. Better yet he didn't even charge me for my "stolen" free lesson.

There used to be a popular comic strip called "Popeye The Sailor Man". The obvious leading character was Popeye himself. One of his supporting characters was, J. Wellington Wimpy who was famous for his love of hamburgers.

His catch phrase was, "I'd gladly pay you on Tuesday for a hamburger today".

Luther shared Wimpy's proclivity of loving hamburgers. His peer group of players insisted he also share the name. He was "Wimpy" ever after.

CONRAD BURKMAN

Conrad, now retired, is the former owner of "The National Billiard News", and for many years was a National Pro Tour referee. Conrad knows where all of the skeletons are buried. Any time I need a new story or an old one verified Conrad is my "Go To Guy". When it comes to telling pool stories, I can spot most guys the seven and the breaks. With Conrad it is "Scratch" at best, and sometimes I have to ask for a little weight, a player at heart, he always spent more time writing and talking about the game than playing it, but he knows the short way around the table with a cue in his hand, and he always knows, "The rest of the story".

Conrad is always in "Story Stroke" and is the best companion I have ever sweated and/or analyzed a pool match with.

GEORGE FELS

I try to read everything that George writes. He is a true aficionado, and a very knowledgeable player. When he writes about it, you get the facts and the emotions of the action. His 'How To" books are well written and professional. My copies are well worn, by frequent use. The BCA Hall Of Fame should make room for this great writer now!!

ROBERT BYRNE

Bob Byrne is a very good Three Cushion Billiard player and one of the best billiard writers in the business. When doing his instructional books and videos, he took the time to, "Get It Right" My respect for Bob grew when it came time to reprint his great book, "Standard Book Of Pool And Billiards".

Gasp, **he actually made corrections**. This exemplary behavior is unheard of in this application. Bob knows his stuff and will share it with all players. If asked, he may also share a story or two.

Robert Byrne has been voted into the B. C. A. HALL OF FAME.

NICK VARNER

This Hall-Of-Fame, World Champion always took a little time to "Talk About The Weather" He is never too busy to chat for a few minutes.

A player I know claimed that Nick said to him, "Doc Rutter is the best pool instructor I know". Thank you Nick, I am honored by your praise.

Here is a tip, if you play straight pool with Nick; you better bring along your "Racking Shoes", and maybe a book or newspaper.

Nick and I were wasting time behind the bleachers at a Minnesota league tournament when he proposed a straight pool game. I lost the lag, broke safe, and then racked five times and on the sixth rack I stated, "Nick I think I am tired of playing Straight Pool. I got to play a couple of safeties up to that point, and we quit with out me ever seeing a pocketable ball.

Hall of Fame players are Tough!

CECIL "BUDDY" HALL

Buddy played everybody that showed up. Not all, but most of them left broke. When he was focused, he was awesome!! **Just don't bring that oversized Bar-Box cue ball with you,** but bring all the cash you can carry!!!!

ROBERT RUNDE

With due respect to all of the great cue makers I know, Bob Runde, all around, is my favorite.

Bob is a master machinist and in the late 80's was a semi-secret partner with another cue maker, Jim McDermott. Due to design style differences, they shortly parted as friends.

Bob next hooked up with Terry Romine, a well-known player and poolroom owner from Milwaukee. That was the birth of the renowned Schon custom cues.

I was hooked; the first time I saw a Schon cue (pronounced Shawn at the factory). An early meeting with Bob created my **New Best Friend**.

Bob reached a retirement point with Schon and semi retired to his secret workshop where he cranks out as many as Five to Twenty five cues per year, when he feels like it. Bob Runde is a solid pool-player but summers on the golf course.

Terry Romine and Evan Clarke however, will still sell you a fine Schon Custom Cue.

I get my personal," Jedi Master", "Light Sabers" from the Secret Runde cave. You have to go through this swamp, behind the woods, and then you have to crawl through a big hollow log full of toads, bats, spiders, and something that slithered over my leg, and licked my foot in the dark but didn't identify itself.

Bob's character, integrity, and artistic design balance, are all reflected in his cue work. He also doesn't use CNC equipment and still assembles high quality sharp points for his cue fronts. The particular Runde cue I use doesn't miss very often, but I had to pay a premium, and **swear to a secret oath**, for that feature.

JIMMY 'THE KID' WETCH

"The Kid" is over forty now. I met Jimmy when he was thirteen, what an experience that was. I could beat him then. When he turned about sixteen I could see the proverbial writing on the wall and left him alone after that.

Jimmy seems hard to please, and that is the base of his pool playing success. When he is at the practice table, you don't see Jimmy slamming balls around. If he is hitting shots, he is dead serious about it. That is the one thing I learned from Minnesota's best player.

When Jimmy was just reaching the peak of his game and was ready to challenge the Pro Tour, such as it was, the tour fell apart and left Jimmy out in the cold.

Jimmy owns "Jimmy's Pro Billiards" in Columbia Heights, Minnesota. We get together once in a while to trade gossip and rumors.

JACKIE GLEASON & PAUL NEWMAN

Jackie Gleason played the fictional "Minnesota Fats" that Walt Tevis created in "The Hustler", a pool character bigger than life, as a protagonist to another figment of Walt's imagination, Paul Newman as "Fast Eddie Felson". These guys were in the back of my mind, with me throughout real and imaginary pool matches. In spite of the rumors to the contrary, these were fictional players. Walt told me that, Face-To-Face, Man-to-Man, in Reno, Nevada, "Doc I made them up from a composite of players I have known". Walt and his wife Eleanor Walker were good company in the "Cheap Seats" of a pool tournament. Yes, I told them a few stories, and shared my tournament pictures with them.

JESSE ENGEL

The future is now. This young man is on his way. In 2010, in Barry Berman's tournament, he beat Earl Strickland on the hill and followed that with a one sided match over Mike Sigal, with an overall finish of, tied for 17th. He was an eighteen years old unknown when he arrived in Virginia. They know him now. Jesse practices at Jerry Johnson's Coon Rapids Billiards, in Minnesota, on a 9 foot Pro-Cut Diamond table. He runs rack after rack of 10-ball and it seems he misses about once or twice per hour. I call him the "Minnesota Whirlwind", he arrives with the evening breeze, makes all the balls in sight, and eases out before the midnight hour, leaving an "It just rained" friendly attitude behind. He has a nice demeanor, and is very focused on his billiard world future. I am a fan already.

PHIL CAPELLE

Phil is a serious energetic author. He wrote a Billiard book each year for seven years. Then he waited about five years and he is releasing, in late 2011 or early 2012, a book about the "last four" in a straight pool rack. Straight pool players should line up for this one. His books are worth reading. Phil is living in the New York City area and is teaching in a couple of the local poolrooms, Society and Amsterdam.

THINGS I LEARNED, JUST WATCHING

Willie Mosconi, mostly played "Short Ball" position, the corner pockets, circled the table and corner-most balls.

Luther Lassiter, used an over wide stance on long shots, and a short grip to practice.

Efren Reyes, never, never, never, lets go of his cue ball. He plays position to a spot on the table on every shot.

Nick Varner, don't play him straight pool, unless you enjoy, racking and watching.

Cecil "Buddy" Hall, He played them all and very few got away with their cash. Buddy knows the value of a good follow through stroke.

Preacher Feeney, players will hold still and listen if you look sincere and use big words, with a wink and a nod, but he could play.

Bert Kinister, if Bert is talking about pool, shut up and listen.

"Fast Freddy" Lamers, if he wants to play Banks, or Billiards, pass.

Wayne "The Rosedale Flash" Miller, if he pulls out his jump cue, don't press the bet. He will play anybody who will provide, "The Right Spot".

Shawn "Double Jump" Oglesbee, just Like Jimmy The Kid, he always played every shot to win. He got his knick name due to a spectacular shot accomplished during one of the Valley State Championship playoffs. Shawn was playing a well-known character from Mankato, Minnesota known as "Big Bird". Shawn, shooting at the *case eight* ball, called a jump over his opponent's ball so the cue ball would come down onto the eight, from above, which would cause the eight ball to jump another of his opponent's balls, and then bounce gaily into the corner pocket. Big Bird was overheard stating, "I just hope he tries that, as it is impossible". Shawn cranked up his focus and calmly stroked home the, "Double Jump" shot to win the match. What about Big Bird? He became Shawn's #1 fan for life. If you meet Shawn's wife, Candice and five children, you will know he is a winner in that area also.

"Princeton Plump", is a player that is hard to find or beat in Kentucky. In the fall of 2010, he went to the Mayo Clinic in Minnesota for some internal rearrangement surgery. I think he was there for facial plastic surgery that would allow him to hide from some bad guy he hustled. You can't fool me PP. No matter what you look like now, I will always recognize the stroke. In the last seventeen years, Like Superman and Clark Kent, "Princeton Plump" and "Denny The Dawg" have never been seen in the same room at the same time?

Irving Crane, always a class act that we all could learn from.

Rudolph Wanderone, another class entirely, but we all loved him.

David Matlock, "The Gunfighter", could miss a shot by 4 inches and would walk back to his chair as if that was exactly what he had planned to do. He will also bank into a side pocket off of the end rails. David is a master with the Bar-Box oversized cue ball and will definitely surprise you at Three Cushion Caroms.

Jimmy Faccine, One of those great "Unknown" players. He has a pool playing rhythm that should be put to music, and is a Magician on the pool table.

Austen "Young Gun" Warner, 2010 VNEA Junior 8-Ball Team, National Champion, This young man is a "Work in Progress", and he plays better by accident than his contemporary, opponents do on purpose. I have been in his ear, but it is hard to make a 16 year old think long range like a 70 year old. He will survive my influence, however. He has great potential. Time will tell.

Tyron R. Wilson, "Down Town Ty" with his intense style of play, led his 8-Ball teams to seven National 8-Ball Championships, in the VNEA and BCA. Ty, your accomplishments have kept Minnesota on the Billiard map. Your teams are a better bet than the Vikings, ha. I have been swapping rumors and pool stories with Ty for 30 years. He is a "Scratch" storyteller and a dedicated player.

Paul A. "Doc" Rutter

Scott Frost, I met him when he was starting out in Olathe Kansas when he would show up at the big tournaments and, with some kind of a spot would take on **anybody, for the cash,** including Efren Reyes. In those days he usually left broke, but he was an "action" player. A few short years later he became a "Derby City " one pocket champion and he doesn't leave broke any more.

Pool Stories I Must Share

Spring Lake Park, Minnesota

"The Rosedale Flash", Wayne Miller, was putting his tack away in Doc's Bohemian Cue, poolroom, when a stranger walks up and states, "I will play you for a hundred dollars a game".

Flash quickly, nods yes, and starts screwing his cue back together. The stranger says, "That's it, without knowing anything about me, you are willing to play for a hundred"?

Wayne replied, "I know everyone in the State that I won't play for a hundred and you aren't one of those". The stranger turned, walked away and was observed shaking his head as he mumbled his way out the door.

Las Vegas, Nevada, the Riviera Casino

The gang is at the Riviera. We were tucked into the slot machines, between the small bar and the Keno counter, Madison's Randy Lamarr, "Down Town" Ty Wilson, Denny "The Dawg" Amundson, Wayne, "The Rosedale Flash", Miller, and of course, "Doc" Rutter. We were all telling various pool lies about bad rolls great shots and such.

A panhandler walks up and says, "Can you help me out fellows. I haven't eaten in two days"?

Randy states loudly, while pointing the way, "Man is you in luck, Kady's Restaurant is right through that door".

If he had known we were pool players, I don't think he would have opened his mouth.

Somerset, Wisconsin, Rendezvous Bar

A local Minnesota short stop, Rotten Roger, is at a Wisconsin bar tournament. During the Calcutta bidding he was run up from $30 to $80 by his out of sight wife before they realized they were bidding against each other. Several players that could see both of them bidding against each other were in a good mood for the rest of the day, Ha.

Somewhere in the USA

Early in Efren Reyes's career, he was being interviewed. When asked, "Is there anyone who you won't play"? He replied, "Nick Varner and Buddy Hall". The interviewer asked, "Are they better than you"? Efren stated, "Oh no, I can beat them, but they are so good, that it just takes too long".

Louisville, Kentucky, the Executive West Hotel

It was the "Derby City Classic" annual tournament and between matches on the exhibition TV table, Billy Incardona and Danny Diliberto are batting around some balls and just "Ragging" on each other. We all know Billy has a good sense of humor and is a master of Poolroom Smart Mouth. Danny "D", no beginner is holding his own and the imaginary score is about even. Johnny Archer arrives and steals the table to get in some practice nine ball. After his break shot the 5 & 6 balls are jawed kind of awkwardly just off of the right side rail, up from the foot of the table about at the third diamond. The balls are angled backwards for a combination shot. So Billy starts in, pretending to talk to Danny, but stealing sidelong glances at Johnny. "Well I don't like his (Johnny's) chances of getting out here, this is not an easy out". Johnny, without a word apparently ignoring Billy, keeps on shooting. Billy, not getting the reaction he expects, continues to rag. "This is a tough out, I think there is trouble here, no sir, and I don't like this run-out at all". Johnny, unperturbed, looking like he is playing in a soundproof glass room, calmly shoots the 4 ball, and plays perfect, let me elaborate, PERFECT , multi rail position, eases the cue ball between the 5 and the 6 ball with the 5 straight in and a table that all the watchers can see is now a "Ray Charles". Johnny glances up. as if noticing Billy for the first time and says, "How do you like it NOW"? Billy realizes he has been out smart mouthed, and the look on his face shows it, says. "Oh well of course, if you want to play it THAT way". Danny and the rail bird were choking back the laughter. Billy found a vacation brochure that demanded his attention.

THE POOLROOM PHILOSOPHY, ADAPTED BY "DOC" RUTTER

Around 1990 I took a couple of previously written lines and by adding a couple of my own, created the "Poolroom Philosophy" here for your enjoyment and further use.

**Don't play pool with a guy, who carries his own chalk,
Don't play cards with a guy named "Doc",
Don't lend your credit card to a blind date,
And don't run seven if you can't run eight.**

Do you want to play for a biscuit or two? RACK-EM.
Do you have a pool story to tell? I'll always listen.

Sincerely, with a sly grin,
Paul A. "Doc" Rutter

CPSIA information can be obtained at www.ICGtesting.com
Printed in the USA
BVOW071527041112

304554BV00001B/40/P